QUEEN LATIFAH

Beastie Boys
Sean Combs
Missy Elliott
Eminem
Jay-Z
LL Cool J
Queen Latifah
Run-DMC
Tupac Shakur
Russell Simmons

QUEEN LATIFAH

Rachel A. Koestler-Grack

QUEEN LATIFAH

Unless otherwise attributed, all quoted material has been taken from Queen Latifah's autobiography, *Ladies First: Revelations of a Strong Woman.*

For information contact:

Chelsea House
An imprint of Infobase Publishing
132 West 31st Street
New York, NY 10001

Library of Congress Cataloging-in-Publication Data

Koestler-Grack, Rachel A., 1973–
Queen Latifah / Rachel A. Koestler-Grack.
p. cm. — (Hip-hop stars)
Includes bibliographical references and index.
ISBN-13: 978-0-7910-9498-3 (hardcover)
ISBN-10: 0-7910-9498-7 (hardcover)
1. Latifah, Queen—Juvenile literature. 2. Rap musicians—United States—Biography—Juvenile literature. I. Title. II. Series.
ML3930.L178K64 2007
782.421649092—dc22
[B] 2007001457

Chelsea House books are available at special discounts when purchased in bulk quantities for businesses, associations, institutions, or sales promotions. Please call our Special Sales Department in New York at (212) 967-8800 or (800) 322-8755.

You can find Chelsea House on the World Wide Web at http://www.chelseahouse.com

Text design by Erik Lindstrom
Cover design by Ben Peterson

Printed in the United States of America

Bang NMSG 10 9 8 7 6 5 4 3 2 1

This book is printed on acid-free paper.

CONTENTS

INTRODUCTION
By Chuck D

Hip-Hop: A Brief History

Like the air we breathe, hip-hop seems to be everywhere. The lifestyle that many thought would be a passing fad has, three decades later, grown to become a permanent part of world culture. Hip-hop artists have become some of today's heroes, replacing the comic book worship of decades past and joining athletes and movie stars as the people kids dream of being. Names like 50 Cent, P. Diddy, Russell Simmons, Jay-Z, Foxy Brown, Snoop Dogg, and Flavor Flav now ring as familiar as Elvis, Babe Ruth, Marilyn Monroe, and Charlie Chaplin.

While the general public knows many of the names, videos, and songs branded by the big companies that make them popular, it's also important to know the holy trinity, the founding fathers of hip-hop: Kool DJ Herc, Grandmaster Flash, and

Afrika Bambaataa. All are deejays who played and presented the records that rappers and dancers delighted themselves upon. Bambaataa single-handedly stopped the gang wars in the 1970s with the themes of peace, unity, love, and having fun.

Hip-hop is simply a term for a form of artistic creativity that was spawned in New York City—more precisely the Bronx—in the early to mid-1970s. Amid the urban decay in the areas where black and Hispanic people dwelled, economic, educational, and environmental resources were depleted. Jobs and businesses were all but moved away. Living conditions were of a lower standard than the rest of the city and country. Last but not least, art and sports programs in the schools were the first to be cut for the sake of lowering budgets; thus, music classes, teaching the subject's history and techniques, were all but lost.

From these ashes, like a phoenix, rose an art form. Through the love of technology and records found in family collections or even those tossed out on the street, the deejay emerged. Different from the ones heard on the radio, these folk were innovating a style that was popular on the island of Jamaica. Two turntables kept the music continuous, with the occasional voice on top of the records. This was the very humble beginning of rap music.

Rap music is actually two distinct words: rap and music. "Rap" is the vocal application that is used on top of the music. On a vocal spectrum, it is between talking and singing and is one of the few alternatives for vocalizing to emerge in the last 50 years. It's important to know that inventors and artists are side by side in the importance of music's development. Let's remember that inventor Thomas A. Edison created the first recording with "Mary Had a Little Lamb" in 1878, most likely in New Jersey, the same state where the first rap recording—Sugarhill Gang's "Rapper's Delight"— was made more than 100 years later, in 1979.

It's hard to separate the importance of history, science, language arts, and education when discussing music. Because of the social silencing of black people in the United States from slavery in the 1600s to civil rights in the 1960s, much sentiment, dialogue, and soul is wrapped within the cultural expression of music. In eighteenth-century New Orleans, slaves gathered on Sundays in Congo Square to socialize and play music. Within this captivity, many dialects, customs, and styles combined with instrumentation, vocals, and rhythm to form a musical signal or code of preservation. These are the foundations of jazz and the blues. Likewise, it's impossible to separate hip-hop and rap music from the creativity of the past. Look within the expression and words of black music and you'll get a reflection of history itself. The four creative elements of hip-hop—emceeing (the art of vocalization); deejaying (the musician-like manipulation of records); break dancing (the body expression of the music); and graffiti (the drawn graphic expression of the culture)—have been intertwined in the community before and since slavery.

However, just because these expressions were introduced by the black–Hispanic underclass, doesn't mean that others cannot create or appreciate hip-hop. Hip-hop is a cultural language used best to unite the human family all around the world. To peep the global explosion, one need not search far. Starting just north of the U.S. border, Canadian hip-hop has featured indigenous rappers who are infusing different language and dialect flows into their work, from Alaskan Eskimo to French flowing cats from Montreal and the rest of the Quebec's provincial region. Few know that France for many years has been the second largest hip-hop nation, measured not just by high sales numbers, but also by a very political philosophy. Hip-hop has been alive and present since the mid-1980s in Japan and other Asian countries. Australia has been a hotbed in welcoming world rap acts, and it has also created its own vibrant hip-hop scene, with the reminder of its government's takeover of indigenous people reflected in every rapper's flow and rhyme. As a rhythm of the people, the continents of Africa and South America (especially Ghana, Senegal, and South Africa, Brazil, Surinam, and Argentina) have long mixed traditional homage into the new beats and rhyme of this millennium.

Hip-hop has been used to help Brazilian kids learn English when school systems failed to bridge the difficult language gap of Portuguese and patois to American English. It has entertained and enlightened youth, and has engaged political discussion in society, continuing the tradition of the African griots (storytellers) and folk singers.

For the past 25 years, hip-hop has been bought, sold, followed, loved, hated, praised, and blamed. History has shown that other cultural music forms in the United States have been just as misunderstood and held under public scrutiny. The history of the people who originated the art form can be found in the music itself. The timeline of recorded rap music spans more than a quarter century, and that is history in itself.

Presidents, kings, queens, fame, famine, infamy, from the great wall of China to the Berlin wall, food, drugs, cars, hate, and love have been rhymed and scratched. This gives plenty reason for social study. And I don't know what can be more fun than learning the history of something so relevant to young minds and souls as music.

Rock the House

The Latin Quarters club in New York City was packed shoulder to shoulder, as it was most nights. It was the mid-1980s, the Golden Age of hip-hop, a new, funky kind of music with thumping beats and cold hard rhymes. The Latin Quarters was the underground circuit for pioneering rappers. Dana Owens, better known to her friends as Princess of the Posse, squeezed her way through the sweaty, pressed bodies on the dance floor. Up on stage, a couple of hip-hop ladies were rocking the house. Dana's eyes came alive. She had never seen female rappers like these before. Sure, she had been there when Salt-N-Pepa first took the stage, all glitzed up in big hair, knee-high boots, and spandex. But these two looked more like the boys in Dana's posse—kickin' it to the crowd in

Queen Latifah worked hard to become hip-hop royalty, honing her craft in friends' basements and small clubs. Latifah has created an entertainment empire, topping music charts and movie bills alike.

Adidas sweat suits and sneakers. Their hair was pulled back in ponytails, just like Dana wore hers sometimes.

Jazzy Joyce was one of the baddest DJs around. She had won the New Music Seminar DJ Competition in 1983 and recorded her first record in 1984. Jazzy Joyce did her thing on the turntables while Sweet T ripped the mic with her rhymes. They were tearing the place up, *and* they were women. Up until this point, Dana hadn't seen female rappers. It was a "male only" hip-hop party, which these girls were crashing.

Dana had been making rhymes of her own, just as a hobby in a friend's basement in New Jersey. Up on stage, doing her thing, the crowd jammin' with her, these thoughts were only pieces of a distant dream. It never really occurred to her that she could play the rap game—until that night. As she watched Jazzy Joyce and Sweet T on stage, she saw them morphing into someone who looked like her. She could see herself up there, spitting out her rhymes, kids going crazy with her beat. She could rock the house. The crowd was chanting her name. That night, she grabbed the possibility and ran with it.

Today, the world knows Dana Owens, Princess of the Posse, as Queen Latifah. At age 18, she may have taken the name "Queen" long before she deserved it. But today, two decades later, she certainly is worthy of royalty. Her debut album, *All Hail the Queen,* is considered one of the best hip-hop albums of all time. She now averages three movies per year in her Hollywood career. She's come a long way from her inner-city roots in the Newark, New Jersey, housing projects. A pioneering female rapper who blazed the way for others to follow, Queen Latifah proved that with a lot of hard work and faith, dreams can become reality.

Tough Girl

Before Queen Latifah even entered the world, her mother knew she would be different. Rita Owens was due to give birth around February 25, 1970. When she hadn't had the baby by the second week of March, the doctors started talking about inducing labor. As soon as the words of this threat were spoken, the future Queen decided it was time to meet the world. Eight-pound-three-ounce Dana Elaine Owens was born on March 18, 1970, to Rita and Lancelot Owens. She had already made a powerful display of her independent nature by refusing to be born before she was ready.

At home in Newark, New Jersey, Dana's older brother waited anxiously to meet his baby sister. His name was Lancelot Hassan Owens Jr., but to the family, he was Winki.

That nickname began when he was a baby, for the way one of his eyes would remain closed when he first woke up from sleeping. According to Queen Latifah's autobiography, *Ladies First: Revelations of a Strong Woman*, Rita would tease, "You winkin' at Mommy? You little Winki." Before long, she was calling him Winki all the time. The nickname stuck with him, even when he was a grown man.

Rita fell head over heels in love with her precious baby girl. She bought a baby book and recorded everything from her first steps to her first words. She treasured Dana's early photographs, her silky newborn hair, and her baby footprints. "I thought of her as my little miracle," Rita recalled. Just before Dana turned a year old, Rita sat down and wrote her daughter a two-page letter. She hoped Dana would read the letter someday and know just how much her mother adored her. "[You] are the most amazing little child I have ever seen," she wrote.

A DYNAMO

Rita quickly learned that there would be no forcing her daughter to be dainty. Dana was her own person. "I got a dynamo," Rita said. Dana's first craze was martial arts. She begged her mother to let her take karate lessons, just like Winki did. Rita was afraid Dana would get hurt. All those rough boys in a big room kicking and punching at each other just didn't seem like the right place for a little girl. But Rita didn't stop her. And unsurprisingly, Dana did a good job holding her own.

Her next phase was a bit more traditional, however. In third grade, she came home from school one day wanting ballet and guitar lessons. Rita was relieved she would no longer have to worry about Dana getting beaten up, but she would have to find a way to afford the lessons. She wanted her daughter to hear "yes" not "no"; she didn't want money to stand in the way of Dana's opportunities. So she found a community center that provided dance and music lessons for a fee that was based on family income.

Before assuming her stage name "Queen Latifah," New Jersey–born Dana Owens had spunk and determination that her mother, Rita, recognized at an early age. Dana had myriad interests, ranging from karate to guitar playing to ballet dancing.

Queen Latifah's parents, Lance and Rita Owens, pose with her at the world premiere of the movie *Beauty Shop*. Though her family has experienced ups and downs, Latifah maintains strong ties with both her mother and father.

Despite Dana's rough-and-tumble exterior, she also possessed an inner daintiness. Her feminine softness was internal. Above all, she was sensitive. If Rita scolded Dana and told her how disappointed she was, Dana would burst into tears. Dana was also compassionate toward others, even if the other was

LOCKED OUT

At times, Dana could be fiercely independent. When she was in kindergarten, she had her first chance to reveal it. Although the school she went to was very good, the neighborhood where it was located was a bit dangerous. After recess, as the kids left the schoolyard and filed back into the building, the teachers would lock the door behind the last child, to ensure everyone's safety. Dana, being the tallest in her class, was always the last in line. One day, she became distracted and wandered away from the other students. Before she knew it, she was locked out of school and stranded, all alone, on the streets of a rough neighborhood.

Unable to get back into the school, Dana headed to the closest safe spot—her grandmother's house, which was a one-and-a-half-mile walk. From High Street, she crossed Broad Street, a major four-lane road, and headed down a long hill. Along the way, a couple of people helped her across the street, but no one thought to ask her why she was out alone in the business district during the middle of the day. It wasn't the best route for walking, but it was the only way she knew. Somehow, at five years old, Dana remembered the car route.

When she got to her grandmother's house, Dana was tired and scared. From inside the house, her grandmother heard a tiny voice crying through the mail slot, "Grandma! Grandma!" The shocked woman let Dana inside and called Rita at work. When she arrived at the house, frantic with worry and relief, she smothered Dana with hugs and kisses. All the while, she just kept telling her, "You are a remarkable little girl. You are something else." At that moment, Rita realized that her daughter could think for herself and handle a difficult situation.

short and furry. At age seven, she brought home a cocker spaniel that she had found while out playing. The dog didn't have a collar or a license. Rita really didn't want the mangy, hyper stray in the house, but Dana insisted. Somehow, the young girl had formed a bond with the dog. So Rita let her keep it. She saw the benefit in letting Dana know what it's like to care for something and have it depend on her.

Dana named the dog Silky. The whole family had to put up with Silky's crazy behavior. He would jump into their car and wouldn't let anyone else get in. He would growl and bark like they were from animal control. When Rita's parents came to visit from Virginia, Silky managed to get into their car. It took them an hour and a half to coax him out. By the end of the ordeal, Dana and her family were all laughing. Her grandparents, however, didn't find it funny. Finally one day, Silky ran away and never returned. Dana was crushed. Even though inwardly Rita was glad to have the dog gone, for Dana's sake, she cried right along with her.

The different traits of Dana's parents influenced her character in complementary ways. While Lancelot brought out the fearless and aggressive side of Dana, Rita was the strong, yet gentle, nurturer. If Dana needed to talk it out, she went to her mother. When the neighborhood kids started calling Dana a tomboy, Rita advised her to tell them, "I'm not a tomboy—I'm just an athlete." Although Rita was tempted to keep Dana inside and protect her from the cruelty of other kids, she knew she couldn't hide Dana from the world. Knowing how rough life can be, she knew Dana would run into a lot of battles in the years ahead. "The best way I could protect her was by showing her how to stick up for herself," she later explained.

SUPERMAN

Lancelot Owens was a Newark cop, a Vietnam veteran, and a karate expert. He was a handsome, smooth-talking tough guy whom Dana looked up to and respected. During her early childhood, Dana idolized her father, referring to him as the strongest, smartest, best-looking man in the world. To her, he was a hero—like Superman.

One day, when Dana was seven years old, her parents took the kids shopping for school clothes in downtown Newark. As they were driving home, they passed a couple on the corner. The man was yelling at the woman, pushing her around and slapping her. (One thing that disgusted Lancelot the most was when men hit women. "Only a punk will raise his hand to a woman," he'd say.) As long as this woman was getting roughed up, he couldn't just drive by, especially with the kids in the back seat yelling, "Daddy, do something!"

Lancelot stopped the car, jumped out, pulled his police gun, and yelled, "Freeze!" He threw the man against a fence and frisked him. Meanwhile, the woman ran away. As soon as the lady was out of sight, Lancelot spun the man around and scolded him about beating a woman. Eventually, he let the man go, but not without a good lecture. It was times like these that made Dana and Winki place their father on a pedestal. But having killed people both as a soldier and a cop, Lancelot had battle scars deep beneath the skin. He wasn't as perfect as Dana believed him to be.

Still, Lancelot taught Dana how to be a strong and confident girl. He believed women should have the same opportunities as men. And given those opportunities, he believed women were capable of achieving the same levels of success as men. He planted that seed in Dana's mind and taught her that she could do anything she wanted to. Most of Lancelot's attitude toward women probably grew from his relationship with his best friend—his older sister, Alita. Alita looked after Lancelot and protected him, so he learned early on that women could be strong and self-reliant. With a tough attitude and her head held high, Alita could really take care of business. If trouble ever crossed her path, there was no doubt she'd be just fine. It was no surprise, therefore, that Lancelot wanted to make sure

Queen Latifah was born in Newark, New Jersey *(above).* When she was 8 years old, she moved with her mother and brother to Newark's inner city housing projects. Though drug use and gang violence were rampant in the projects, Latifah and her brother lived a happy childhood.

his daughter could take care of herself, too. He didn't want to have to worry about her.

When Dana was with her father, she would jump fences and climb trees. Soon, she followed Winki out to play baseball and basketball. Rita tried to dress her in pretty outfits, with bows in her hair and matching bobby socks. But by the end of the day, the bows would be missing or bumped to the side, and her socks would scrunched down and dirty. She would have dried chocolate in the corners of her mouth and grass stains on her dress. Oftentimes, she came home all scraped up with bruises on her knees. Lancelot simply smiled and teased, "Your legs are too pretty to have those marks on them." But Dana didn't care about the cuts and scratches. She was having fun being brave and daring. She wore the bruises and scrapes as the marks of a fearless girl.

Because the Owenses lived in Newark, Dana rarely spent time in the countryside or secluded forests. When she was six, her dad gave her a chance to see what life was like outside their concrete jungle. He took Dana, Winki, and their cousins camping for the first time at the Delaware Water Gap. It rained all weekend, but Lancelot made them tough it out. "Hey, life's not always going to be sunshine every day," he said. "What are you going to do when there are a few clouds? You have to keep going." The kids helped pitch the tent and set up camp. They experienced the real outdoors. Their bathroom was the woods, and they cooked their meals over an open fire. One day, they ate dehydrated eggs. The next morning, they ate Frosted Flakes with water instead of milk. Lancelot woke the children before dawn so they could see that the sun rises in the east. As they hiked through the woods, Dana's dad taught them that moss grows on the north side of the trees. They learned—the itchy, painful way—how to identify poison ivy. They even smoked out insects.

At times, it was hard for Dana to stay in a tent with a bunch of guys. But she was too young to know any of society's beliefs that girls were not tough. She stuck it out, and there was tremendous glory at the end, knowing she had gone days without running water or a roof over her head. She was proud of her concrete endurance and was eager to find out what else she could conquer.

I ONLY HAVE EYES FOR YOU

Rita had a much different upbringing than Lancelot. Although they both came from large families, she was a country girl,

When she was a young girl, Queen Latifah loved to sing and dance, a passion that led her as a teenager to the hip-hop clubs of New York City. Inspired by the female acts, Latifah was determined to make a career of her passion.

the daughter of a military sergeant, Henry Bray, and his wife, Catherine. She lived in a comfortable home on an army base in Arlington, Virginia. Her backyard was Arlington Cemetery. Each morning, she woke up to 5:00 reveille. She was the middle of seven children, but she was the youngest girl. Therefore, her parents were overprotective of her. They didn't let her do much, except to sing with her sister, Angel. During a slice of time away from the watchful eye of Sergeant Bray, she met Lancelot Owens.

At the time, Lancelot was a soldier in the Honor Guard. On the base, there was a club where young people could go to sing and dance. One afternoon, Lancelot and some of his buddies were in the club's piano room, singing tunes from the Temptations and the Four Tops. Lancelot had his own little singing group called the Grand Prix Machine. As they were "doo-wopping" to "I Only Have Eyes for You," Rita and Angel walked in and asked if they could sing backup. Only sixteen years old, Rita didn't even know the old song from the 1940s. But she improvised. By the time the song was over, Rita and Lancelot were in love.

In those days, Rita seemed to fall in love every week, but usually from afar. She was a dreamy teenager who longed for adventure and romance. With Lancelot, she had finally found both. He was a strong, handsome man who walked with a cool strut and had a smooth way of talking. His "northern" accent and Newark slang excited Rita's young Virginia ears. In an instant, she was swept off her feet.

Rita married Lancelot, left her friends and family in Virginia, and moved to Newark, New Jersey. She took a chance, moving to a new town and building a new life. A year later, she gave birth to Winki, and two years after that, she had Dana. By twenty, she had a husband and two babies to care for. She had crossed the bridge from girlhood to womanhood. However, the thrill of marrying the most fascinating and exciting man quickly faded when she realized every man in Newark walked with a strut and spoke with an accent. But she loved being a mother, and nothing could take that away from her.

Together, Rita and Lancelot laid a solid foundation for Dana and Winki. Lancelot was the driven parent, taking no nonsense, while Rita was always there to listen and encourage. Their personalities made for a perfect balance and harmony in the household, one that Dana thought would last forever.

Bombshell

When Dana was eight years old, her mother and father sat her and Winki down in the living room of their Shely Street apartment for a family meeting. Dana curiously studied their grim faces. She could tell it was serious. It was 1978. Kids were jamming to groups like Earth, Wind & Fire. Bell-bottoms, beads, and Afros were the "in" fashions. Dana and Winki were rolling along without a care in the world. Then their parents dropped a bombshell. Queen Latifah recounts the episode in *Ladies First.*

"Your father and I are separating," Rita said. "When two people stay together for a long time, sometimes they have problems. And sometimes those problems can only be worked out separately."

"It has nothing to do with y'all," Lancelot added. "I will be there for you. Your mother and I just need some space apart."

As far as Dana knew, her mother and father made a perfect couple. She had rarely seen them argue. In Dana's eyes, they were the ideal family—mother, father, brother, and sister. They even had a family dog—a German shepherd mix. Soon, Dana learned that things aren't always what they seem.

Lancelot was great at pretending everything was fine, but inside he was a mess. Every day he carried the pain and torment from his years in the Vietnam War. In Vietnam, he had shot people and was shot at day after day for two and a half years. When he returned home, he did not receive a hero's welcome. Instead, the soldiers were booed. Eventually, he turned to drugs to numb the pain. He began looking to other women for love and comfort.

Rita and the kids packed their things and moved out. Years later, Dana realized how much courage it took her mother to leave. Rita had given up her entire life for Lancelot. Before they met, she had been accepted to Howard University and Spelman College. Instead of going to school, she married Lancelot and moved "up north." She left a comfortable home in Virginia for the cold cement of New Jersey. Now, she was starting over again.

Although Dana and Winki knew their father had a few lady friends, it wasn't until years later that they learned he had also fathered children with some of them. At first, Dana wondered, "Weren't we enough to keep him happy? He needed something better?" No matter how irrational these thoughts were, Dana couldn't stop them from crossing her mind and tearing away her self-confidence. Even worse, she lost respect for her father—the man who was once her hero. His actions shook her confidence in men. For a long time, she couldn't trust any men.

Dana never talked to her father about what he did to the family and to his other children. One day, she wrote him a long letter, asking why he had cheated on her mother. She

Earth, Wind & Fire ***(above, in the 1970s)*** **was a favorite group of Queen Latifah's when she was a child. In many ways, soul groups laid the musical foundation for hip-hop, which began its ascent in the mid-to-late 1970s.** ***(Front row, from left):*** **Al McKay, Philip Bailey, Maurice White, Verdine White and Larry Dunn.** ***(Back row, from left):*** **Ralph Johnson, Andrew Woolfolk and Johnny Graham.**

wrote, "Look at the future and the beautiful kids you've produced and be something. They need you. The world is tough enough; kids need their fathers." But she never mailed it. She was too angry with him.

Still, deep down Dana loved her father and thought about him often. As time passed, her anger lessened, and she began wondering if she should forgive him. One day, Dana talked to her friend Monifa about it. Monifa's father had passed away when she was nine. After listening to Dana complain about her dad, Monifa said, "At least you have your father." Those words had an impact on Dana. She decided that Monifa was right: at least her father was still alive. As long as Dana's dad was around, she still had a chance to fix their relationship.

Finally, she accepted the fact that she could not control what her father did. And as much as she tried to convince herself that she didn't need her father, she knew she really did. At last, she decided to focus on what she could control—her own choices. She could choose to have Lancelot in her life. She could decide to forgive him and hold on to the good memories she had of him.

Her vision of a superman dad had shattered in front of her. Lancelot Owens was not the person Dana had built him up to be. But she could decide to accept who he was and embrace the good he was capable of offering to her. As she remembers in *Ladies First*, she made a list of the things she could do to mend their relationship:

1. I can continue to make the choice to have my father in my life now.
2. I can talk to him regularly so that we never again lose touch with who the other person is.
3. I can start to see him as a human being, not as a superman who is always falling short of my expectations.
4. I can remind myself that as time passes, wounds heal.

Finally, Dana made the choice to love her father.

THE PROJECTS

The most dramatic change Dana faced was moving. The family had just moved into a lovely garden apartment on Leslie Street in Hillside, New Jersey. Now, they had to move again. Rita, Winki, and Dana settled in the Hyatt Court housing project a few miles away. Up until this point, they had always been upgrading, moving to a better place, a better neighborhood. Dana had lived in four different apartments before she was eight, but each time had been a step up. This time, things were different. The move wasn't to a nicer apartment.

The project consisted of several three-story brick buildings in the East Ward of Newark. The back walls of each building faced each other to form a triangle, inside which was a courtyard where residents hung out. Dana's third-floor bedroom looked out to the courtyard. Many days, Dana would stare

THE PROJECTS

Hyatt Court is a public housing complex in Newark's Ironbound section, a poor, working-class neighborhood circled by railroad tracks. Dana and her family called Hyatt Court "the projects." Housing projects usually consist of a block of apartment buildings owned by a government agency. Often, these types of residences are simply referred to as "projects." The goal of projects is to create affordable housing for low-income families.

Unfortunately, these types of apartments were usually built in dangerous, poverty-stricken neighborhoods. Many of these buildings were poorly managed and inadequately maintained. Over the years, projects gained a reputation for gangs and violence, drug use and drug trafficking, prostitution, and other crimes.

The U.S. government has passed numerous laws in an effort to clean up projects around the country and attract tenants with a wider range of income levels.

out the window at the people down below. With the window cracked, she listened to the music, the dogs barking, children laughing and playing, and people arguing. There was always activity down there, at all hours of the day.

Rita let Dana and Winki decorate their rooms however they wanted. Winki's room was cluttered with Tyco racing cars and tracks. He barely had room to walk, but he didn't care. On the other hand, Dana's room was open and bare. She slid her bed against the window, where she could comfortably spy onto the courtyard, and arranged her dolls neatly on top of it. In the corner, she had a small table, always set for afternoon tea. Off to the side, she kept her stereo—an eight-track player—and her favorite music. The open space in the center of the room was perfect for singing and dancing.

Outside, Hyatt Court looked like any other inner-city complex. The barren steps that led into the buildings were dusted with soot and layered in grime. Car horns blared on the streets, and residents hung out on the courtyard sidewalks. But inside apartment 3K, Rita had created a whole other world. Just inside the front door, she had placed a small bowl of potpourri on a table. The minute Dana walked into the apartment, she would take a deep breath of the sweet, delicate smell rising from the table. Rita chose pretty throw rugs to cover holes and stains on the carpets. She sewed curtains for the windows and pillow covers for the living room chairs. She found a sheet of brightly colored cloth at a discount store and used it to cover the couch. Rita had a magic touch when it came to decorating.

Most important, Rita wanted apartment 3K to feel like their space away from a crazy world. She knew the kids needed a comfortable haven from all the changes that were happening in their lives. She made sure their home had dignity and respect. "She created an environment where we could come together at the dinner table every night and look around and say a prayer for the abundance we had in our home," Dana later said. "We would focus on what we had inside, not on the barren landscape that made up Hyatt Court." Even years later, having her own special space is important to Dana. If she has to rent a house in Los Angeles while working on a movie there, she finds a way to bring her style into it—with candles, incense, and pictures of her family and friends. It has to feel like a home.

There was no shame in living at Hyatt Court. But growing up in the inner city can make a child feel dishonorable. Rita worked hard to make sure her children didn't fall into that trap. She pointed out that dishonor comes from being inconsiderate of one's neighbors, a lack of ambition, and giving up hope for a better life. Negative talk seemed to run up and down the hallways at Hyatt Court, and Rita made it her mission to keep that attitude locked out of their apartment. "Just because you're living in the projects," she told the kids, "doesn't mean you're *of* the projects." To her, Hyatt Court was not a permanent home; it was merely a stepping-stone on a road to her goal. She had plans to attend and finish college so that she could find a good job and give her children something better.

While they were living at the projects, however, Rita made the best of the situation. She even tried to bring a sense of hope to other childing living there, organizing field trips for the entire building. They took bus rides to Wildwood, New Jersey, and other areas along the Jersey shore, and to museums in Manhattan and the Bronx Zoo. Rita knew how important it was for kids to venture out of their environment. She believed children needed to explore beyond the boundaries of their neighborhoods, even if it was just a park in a different neighborhood. When Dana and Winki gazed out the bus window, Rita wanted them to see the world as a huge place with lots of opportunities.

Above all else, Rita did not want her children to feel like Hyatt Court was their destiny. "Look, you're black; you're already at a disadvantage," she told them. "You have to work twice as hard to make it. So don't get too comfortable here." To make sure they saw a different perspective, every summer Rita took Dana and Winki to Maryland and Virginia where Rita's family owned a

Queen Latifah's bond with Rita Owens goes beyond that of mother and daughter. They respect each other as women and they find solace in each other as friends. In the photograph above, Queen Latifah introduces Rita to a high school audience at the New Jersey Performing Arts Center, where Latifah spoke and answered questions from students.

big house surrounded by streams, pecan trees, and fruit bushes. Unlike Newark pools, the swimming pools down South were filled with clean water and weren't crammed with hundreds of kids. People smiled and were polite. Dana's cousins answered "Yes, ma'am" and "No, sir." They went to church every Sunday. And every meal seemed like a Thanksgiving feast.

When they returned home at the end of August, the neighborhood kids seemed so different. Dana and Winki had just spent a summer jam-packed with fun activities and friends. Suddenly, it wasn't enough just to hang out in the courtyard, doing nothing. Instead, they spent time at the recreation center across the street, playing cards, Uno, Trouble, Monopoly, Ping-Pong, Connect Four, and Othello. "Looking back," Dana commented years later, "we barely noticed that we lived in the projects."

On Their Own

Without Dana's dad around, life was harder for the family. But Rita never let the kids know how tough things really were. She took a couple of extra jobs to help pay the bills and managed to keep the kids in private Catholic schools. For several years, she worked tirelessly juggling jobs and family obligations. She got off the late shift at the Newark Post Office at 7:00 in the morning, hurried home, made breakfast for Dana and Winki, and took them to school. Then, she rushed to the Holiday Inn at Newark Airport, where she waited tables until 2:00 P.M., just in time to pick up the kids from school, cart them home, and cook dinner.

When Rita started classes at Kean College (now Kean University), she loaded the kids in the car and took them to

LATIFAH'S LAWS: LOVE YOURSELF

Latifah begins her autobiography by saying, "I am not a psychologist or a sociologist." She doesn't have any degrees that make her an expert on life. Nevertheless, her book offers some incredible insights for young and old alike. She is a young black woman from the inner city who has made it, despite the odds. Many people would find Latifah's Laws worth listening to. One law gravitates around self-image and the importance of finding love for one's self. She writes:

"People look at me now and think, 'Wow, there's a full-sized woman who has it together.' Puh-lease! It took me years to get to the point where I loved my body. And I truly do love my body. But I had to go through stages. I hated my breasts. I hated my butt. I even hated the way I walked. Some girls, with no effort, can just walk cute and ladylike. Not me. I had this lumbering stride that would kind of end up on my toes when I took a step. . . .

"Television, the movie industry, the fashion corps tell us that [the] skin-and-bones look is beautiful. . . . [T]he message that comes through loud and clear is that we need to be thinner, yet bigger-breasted, that we need to flatten our stomachs, lighten our skin, and fill our lips with collagen. We need shorter/longer hair and less of this and more of that.

"I could never fit into the clothes that brighten glossy magazines. But I also hated those 'large-size' stores, with half-sizes and X-sizes and dress sizes that went up to senior-citizen ages. I thought the styles were ugly and made me look like an old lady. So I began looking for my own touch and started wearing clothes that fit my personality.

"You are the only standard you need. You shouldn't want to look like anybody but you. God made you. And my mother always told me, 'God don't make junk.'"

Among Queen Latifah's most important ideals are pride in identity and believing in one's self. She believes that all people, especially women, should embrace their unique qualities. Here, she stands on Capitol Hill in Washington, D.C., during the first annual National Women's Confidence Day.

class with her. On some nights, the woman who cleaned classrooms would take the children along on her rounds so Rita could concentrate on her schoolwork. Everybody on campus knew Dana and Winki. They were given candy and treats, and they collected balls from the field after lacrosse practice. Before this time, Dana and Winki had never even heard of lacrosse.

Sometimes, they were allowed to bring the balls back to the neighborhood to play.

After class, Rita tried to grab a few hours of sleep before her shift at the post office. For an entire year, she averaged two to three hours of sleep a night. But by the end of it all, she had saved enough money for a down payment on a cute blue house on Central Avenue and Twelfth Street in Newark. The house was small—nothing elaborate—but it would be theirs. All she needed was a $40,000 mortgage from the bank. Because she had no credit history, the bank refused the loan. Rita must have been crushed, but she didn't let it discourage her.

When they moved into Hyatt Court, Rita had promised the children they would not live in the projects forever. Since they couldn't have a house, she shifted to Plan B—an apartment on Littleton Avenue. They rented the second floor of a three-family house in a residential area of Newark. The new apartment seemed like a palace, with huge rooms and a big backyard. This house would be the place where Dana would spend most of her teenage years.

About this time, Rita started dating again. She was careful about bringing men around the house because Dana and Winki still missed their dad. Rita didn't want to hurt their feelings. On occasion, however, she invited someone to dinner or back to the house after an evening out. One night, Dana and Winki discovered a tiny hole in Dana's bedroom wall. On the other side of this wall was the living room. The hole didn't go all the way through, but being nosy, Dana took a steak knife and dug the rest of the way out. Now the hole was big enough to see everything going on in the living room. Dana and Winki took turns watching Rita and her boyfriend, who were sitting on the couch talking. Suddenly, the man gave Rita a deep kiss.

Dana was crushed. This man wasn't her father. It didn't seem right that he should be getting so close to her mother. When her parents split up, Rita told her, "Mommy and Daddy are separating." Rita had not mentioned that she might see other men. Dana figured that "separating" meant her mom and dad were just taking a little break from each other. She didn't realize her parents were actually divorced.

After her date left, Rita came into Dana's room to say good night. Both Dana and Winki were sitting on the bed in tears because they saw a man who wasn't their father kissing their mom. Rita immediately noticed the hole in the wall. At first, they were in trouble for wrecking the new apartment. Then, she sat down and talked to them. She explained that she was a single woman now, and it was okay for her to date other men. She told them that she needed to go out and enjoy life, too.

At the time, Dana and Winki only saw her as their mother. They didn't see her as Rita Bray Owens—a woman with her own interests and needs. They needed her to explain that she wasn't just a mother; she was a woman. That day, Dana learned an important lesson: The only person in her life she can control is herself. As much as she'd like to, she can't make choices for someone else.

Even though Rita had taught her kids an important lesson, she'd learned something important, too. Rita cared deeply about her children's feelings, maybe even more than her own. After that night, she rarely brought anyone home with her.

PLAYING HOOKY

Most of the time, Rita sacrificed for her children and rarely took a break to pamper herself. On one occasion, however, shortly after the divorce, she and a group of friends took a two-week vacation in France. Dana and Winki stayed with Lancelot's sister, Elaine, and their uncle Buddy, on North Fifteenth Street in East Orange, New Jersey. At the time, the kids were attending a Catholic grammar school—St. Aloysius—in Newark near Hyatt Court. They had a strict schedule to follow to get to school and back home again. They were supposed to get up at 6:00 in the morning, eat breakfast, and take the bus

When they were children, Dana and her older brother, Winki, played hooky from their New Jersey private school and used their lunch money to take a train into Manhattan. Young Dana would often look to her older brother for guidance, companionship, and entertainment.

to Penn Station in downtown Newark. Then, they would take a train to St. Aloysius. Aunt Elaine gave each of them about five dollars every day, enough money to get to school, buy lunch, and take the bus back home at the end of the day.

On the first day, Winki came up with another idea. He read the schedule at Penn Station and saw that they could catch a train to New York City. They had tagged along on outings to Manhattan with their parents plenty of times before, but they had no inkling about how to get around the city on their own. Still, Winki saw that as an adventure too tempting to pass up. He wanted to play hooky from school.

"Let's ride to the World Trade Center," he suggested to Dana.

"Okay," Dana replied. And off they went.

The two of them took the train to the World Trade Center and rode the elevator more than one hundred stories up to the observation deck. Another group of kids was on a class trip, so Dana and Winki tried to blend in with them. They must have stuck out a little bit, however, wearing their St. Aloysius uniforms. After that, they paraded around lower Manhattan and bought a couple of hot dogs with their lunch money. They hiked back to Penn Station just in time to catch a ride home, and walked through the door of Aunt Elaine's house without arousing any suspicions.

The next day, Winki wanted to do it again. It was the first time either one of them had done something so forbidden and got away with it. They got hooked on playing hooky. But by Friday, Dana was getting bored of the routine. There was nothing left to see at the World Trade Center, and she was getting sick of eating hot dogs. She began missing her teacher and friends. During the morning train ride, Dana popped the news. She did not want to cut class anymore.

"I'm going anyway," Winki protested. He refused to get off the train at the St. Aloysius stop. Dana was furious with him, but she stayed on the train, too. She couldn't very well go to school by herself. The teachers would certainly ask where she had been all week, and where Winki was today. It was their last day of footloose and fancy-free behavior, however. When they got home that night, they found out that the school had called. The jig was up. And they were in big trouble.

When Uncle Buddy asked whose idea it was to skip school, Dana was quick to point the finger at Winki. Moments later, Dana probably regretted tattling on her brother. Buddy gave Winki a good "whupping." While Dana listened to Winki hollering in the other room, she was filled with rage. "Who was Uncle Buddy to touch my brother?" she thought. The punishment may have fit the crime, but Dana believed Buddy should

When Dana and Winki escaped to Manhattan for their secret adventure, they visited the World Trade Center (WTC) and feasted on hot dogs. Here, visitors to the 107th floor observation deck at the WTC look out over New York Bay. Tragically, the World Trade Center's north and south towers collapsed as a result of the September 11, 2001, terrorist attacks.

have called their father to deal it out. That night, Dana and Winki plotted again. They called Lancelot after everyone had gone to bed and told him what had happened. The next day, Lancelot had a long talk with Uncle Buddy about disciplining his kids. Once again, Dana and Winki were a team.

Growing up, Winki was one of Dana's best friends, and not just because they were brother and sister. They learned from an early age to lean on each other and encourage each other. Winki was Dana's protector, and with Lancelot gone, she looked to him as the man of the house. She always wanted her big brother there to share every laugh and every tear.

Princess of the Posse

In the late 1970s, Muslim names were popular across the country, especially in Newark. Perhaps it was because the late African-American leader Malcolm X and the Nation of Islam had made a comeback in popularity among young people. Maybe it grew from the black revolutionaries and the Black Panther movement that led civil unrest in Newark neighborhoods. In any case, many of Dana's friends had taken Muslim names—Malik, Rasheedah, and Shakim. Even Winki became inspired, taking the name Jameel. So at age eight, Dana thought it was her turn to choose a name.

Dana wanted to pick a name that represented who she was. In her mind, the name *Dana* was sister, daughter, friend, and student. She wanted a name that was all hers, not defined

During the late 1970s, many of Dana's friends changed their American names to reflect their Muslim heritage, prompting Dana to do the same. After looking through a book of names, she found the perfect one to epitomize her spirit: "Latifah," which means "delicate, sensitive, kind." Little did Latifah know that this name would one day be famous.

by someone else's expectations. Her cousin Sharonda owned a book of Muslim names, with the meaning listed next to each one. One day, she and Sharonda went through the book. Sharonda picked Salima Wadiah for her name. Mamoud was already her last name, so she became Salima Wadiah Mamoud. Next, it was Dana's turn. She was filled with excitement and anticipation as she thumbed through the pages of the book. She saw many names she liked, like Aisha and Kareemah, before she came to Latifah. She loved the way it sounded, the way it rolled off her tongue. Then, she read what it meant—"delicate, sensitive, and kind." Dana thought it fit her perfectly. It made her feel feminine and special. Even though she played basketball, softball, and kickball, she was delicate on the inside. She wanted to show a little bit of that on the outside with her new name.

Choosing a name was just one step on the road to discovering herself. In the early 1980s, she entered Irvington High School. Her high school years opened her eyes to a whole new craze, a music culture that beat in her blood.

THE LATIN QUARTERS

The Latin Quarters club once stood on the corner of Forty-eighth Street and Broadway in New York City's Times Square. When Latifah was a young teenager, Times Square was marred with shady movie theaters, peep shows, fake-ID shops, shifty characters, and danger. Today, Times Square has been tidied up; it attracts tourists and families to its stores and theaters. A Sheraton hotel has taken over the spot where Latifah and her friends once congregated at the Latin Quarters.

The Latin Quarters pulsed with excitement. Rappers such as Grandmaster Flash, Salt-N-Pepa, Run-DMC, and the Beastie Boys took the stage with their baggy jeans, sweat suits, and a funky beat that was new to Latifah. Dancers bopped in the center of the floor, surrounded by a crowd fifty people deep. It was a rush like nothing Latifah had ever felt before. To get into the

Latin Quarters, Latifah sometimes had to stand in a line that wrapped around the block. Before she paid her ten-dollar admission, she had to be frisked—or pat searched—by security. She never liked being frisked (it made her feel violated) but once she made it through the doors of the club, she forgot all about it. The music, the dancers, the rappers, they all captivated her.

Rap was the newest music to hit the scene. Almost overnight, rap became the common language of the youth of America. It was more than just music, more than even communication. Rap was an expression, an attitude, and a culture. This new music phenomena transcended ethnic and racial barriers. Young people were getting the chance to voice their opinions, and the world was paying attention to them—from other hip-hoppers to the mainstream public to the hot shots at the record companies. And Latifah was right there in the thick of it. She was one of the people making the culture. "It was amazing to be a part of such a force," she later said. "We hit like the Coney Island Cyclone—just as wild and just as shaky."

At this time, Latifah was working at the Burger King on High Street in Newark. This job helped her afford her "hip-hop education." It is also where she met her friends Hakim and Bree. Hakim once dated a girl who worked with Latifah, and he and Bree would always hang out at Burger King, waiting for her to get off work. Hakim and Bree were taggers, or graffiti artists. Back then, graffiti was a real art—not just putting your initials, or tags, on a subway car. Real taggers, like Hakim and Bree, made bold statements with their art, and Latifah thought their work was cool. More importantly, they were the ones who first took Latifah to the Latin Quarters and introduced her to the world of hip-hop.

On Saturday nights, Hakim and Bree would meet Latifah at Burger King after she got off work around 11:00. In the restaurant bathroom, she would change out of her brown, orange, and yellow uniform into her hip-hop gear. Usually, she wore a Swatch sweat suit, a pair of K-Swiss sneakers, some scrunchy Guess socks, a fisherman's hat, and a backpack to carry her Burger King clothes. With the hip-hop outfit came a whole new attitude. No one could tell her what to think or what to do. She was cool. The only things missing were the big gold bamboo earrings everyone was wearing. Latifah couldn't afford gold.

The music was a lure for Latifah. She lived for the dark, loud, crowded dance floors. Even the bathrooms were packed. The big-dog rappers like Run-DMC and Kool Moe Dee would perform at the Latin Quarters on a regular basis. And they didn't just run the stage. They would be down in the crowd, getting

HIP-HOP

Hip-hop, also called rap, is a style of popular music that emerged in the mid-1970s but hit the mainstream public in the mid- to late 1980s. The music contains two main elements—rapping, or emceeing, and deejaying, or mixing and scratching records. Together with hip-hop dancing, better known as break dancing, and urban-inspired art, often called graffiti, these four elements make up hip-hop—a cultural movement initiated by inner-city youth, mostly African Americans in New York City.

Typically, hip-hop consists of one or more rappers who tell semi-autobiographic tales. The lyrics are intensely rhythmic and make heavy use of poetic techniques like assonance, alliteration, and rhyme. The rapper is accompanied by an instrumental track—or beat—performed by a DJ. Beats are often created by using a sample of the percussion break of another song—usually of a funk or soul recording. In addition to beat, other sounds are sometimes sampled or synthesized.

their dance on. In addition to the Latin Quarters, Latifah found her way to underground clubs in Brooklyn, house and block parties in the Bronx, and hangouts in Harlem. Sometimes she went to the Newark clubs, like Zanzibar and Sensations, but they mainly played club music. That wasn't the scene for Latifah anymore; she was all about hip-hop.

Still, Latifah was too young to be going to New York City all alone and hanging out all night. Many nights, she kept her mother awake and worrying about her. One evening, Latifah made plans to go to the Latin Quarters with her friend Gloria. Gloria was twenty-one—like many of her friends, much

Hip-hop took shape in the New York City borough of the Bronx when DJs began isolating the percussion break from funk and disco songs. Originally, the role of the MC was to introduce the DJ and the music and to keep the crowd excited. MCs would talk between songs, tell jokes and anecdotes, and pump up people to dance. Gradually, this job became more stylized and turned into rapping. By 1979, hip-hop had transformed into a commercially popular music genre.

In the 1990s, a form of hip-hop called gangsta rap became a major part of American music, causing heated controversy. Many people thought gangsta rap lyrics promoted violence, promiscuity, and drug use. Nevertheless, by the beginning of 2000, hip-hop remained a staple of popular music and was being performed around the world. In 2006, rap music was the second most popular form of music in the United States, after classical music.

older than Latifah. On the way, Gloria wanted to stop at her boyfriend's house. The night ticked away, and it became obvious that they wouldn't be going to the club. Latifah couldn't go alone because she only had a dollar. Gloria had promised to pay Latifah's way. But Gloria refused to leave, and Latifah had the itch to hear hip-hop.

By midnight, she realized she wouldn't make it home that night. Knowing she was in trouble already, she was too scared to call her mother. As each hour passed, Latifah knew her mother must be growing more and more worried. Usually when Latifah went out, she would quietly sneak back into the house before anyone woke up. Often, Winki and Rita wouldn't even notice she had been out so late. This time, the sun was up and the streets were busy before she was heading home. Finally around noon, she tip-toed up the stairs to their apartment door. She gently nudged the key into the keyhole, praying that her mom and Winki were sleeping in late that day. When she opened the door, Winki was waiting for her.

"What's wrong with you, Dana?" he yelled, inches away from her face. "Don't you know Mommy was up all night crying?" Rita had spent the night calling all the hospitals in the area and had checked with all Dana's friends, the police station, and even the local morgue. Winki was livid with how inconsiderate Latifah had been.

Latifah felt rotten. She was so concerned about making it to the club, and then about getting in trouble, that she had lost sight of everything else. She hadn't taken a minute to think about how her mother was feeling. Latifah hurried into Rita's bedroom. Rita threw her arms around Latifah, sobbing. Over and over, she told Latifah that she loved her. By this time, Latifah was crying, too. Rita was so relieved that her daughter was safe, she wasn't angry anymore. "I just ask one thing," she pleaded. "Please let me know you're all right. Just take a minute, call collect or whatever and just tell me you're safe so that

Latifah's interest in hip-hop was fueled by her visits to the Latin Quarters club in Manhattan's Times Square. Prominent acts included Run-DMC, Salt 'N' Pepa, and the Beastie Boys. These cutting-edge performers inspired Latifah and allowed her to envision herself onstage, commanding the crowd just like them.

I don't stay up all night worried." From then on, Latifah always made sure her mother knew exactly where she was.

GO RAMSEY

Latifah was doing more than just soaking in the hip-hop culture. She was spreading it. Her friends didn't leave New Jersey that often, but Latifah couldn't be kept away from New York.

Kool Moe Dee *(right, with producer Fred Jerkins in 2000)*, an early hip-hop standout, was born in Manhattan and known for his eclectic rhymes and freestyle abilities. He was a pioneer of the "battle rap" style, in which two or more rappers face off and try to defeat each other by way of their MC skills.

Her friends, or posse, depended on her to bring back some of that New York flavor each week. Every night, Latifah shuttled clothing styles, dances, and fresh lingo through the Lincoln Tunnel between New York and New Jersey.

There was another person who was bringing hip-hop to Irvington High, a young man named Ramsey. Latifah first heard of Ramsey from her friend Sandy Hill, who dated him for a while. The girls lived across the street from each other, and every afternoon, Latifah got a complete update on what Sandy and Ramsey had done the day before. Latifah had never known anyone named Ramsey, so she remembered the name. He was a bold immigrant from Liberia who lived in his own apartment and attended Irvington High as a nineteen-year-old junior.

When Latifah first started going to high school, hip-hop fashions—the baggy, low-slung jeans; boots; oversized T-shirts; and baseball caps—were not in style. Instead, kids wore designer labels—Calvin Klein, Polo, Ralph Lauren, and Gucci. But Ramsey had his own style. He went to Greenwich Village in New York City to buy his clothes. Everybody in New Jersey was talking about the Village, but Ramsey had actually been there, scoping out the scene and collecting the look that all of Irvington High wanted a piece of. He was a trendsetter. He was one of the first people, besides Latifah, to hit the clubs in Manhattan, like the Palladium, the Garage, and the Roxy.

Ramsey and Latifah finally crossed paths one day on the football field. Latifah was heading to gym class, and Ramsey was coming off the field on his way to English class. Latifah heard someone yell, "Yo, Ramsey!" So she quickly spun around to get a look at this person she'd heard so much about. From the way Sandy described him, Latifah expected to lay eyes on an incredibly handsome man. Instead, she saw a scrawny, bony-elbowed, dark-skinned boy in a leather cap, jeans, and the latest Adidas shell tops. "That's Ramsey?" she thought out loud.

Latifah walked up to him and introduced herself as a friend of Sandy's. "She used to talk about you all the time," Latifah said. "I know everything about you." The two of them instantly clicked. Latifah was impressed by his hip-hop knowledge. He knew the music and was in with all the DJs. He was at every party. If he liked the music, Ramsey would rip off his shirt like he had the muscles of Arnold Schwarzenegger and dance harder, swinging his shirt in the air over his head. Within seconds, the crowd would be circled around him, chanting, "Go, Ramsey! Go Ramsey!" Ramsey's apartment soon became home base for Latifah and her hip-hop posse. There, he'd fill them in on the latest music and clothing. Next to Winki, he was Latifah's best friend.

Ramsey didn't rhyme or deejay, but he knew how to direct and critique other people. At his apartment, people would give their best rap and wait for his approval or criticism. It was like going to rap school.

Even though Ramsey knew the DJs, oddly, it was Latifah's mother who put her in contact with the one DJ who would change her life. Rita was in charge of activities at Irvington High School. She was the one to line up DJs for class parties. One day, she introduced Latifah to Mark the 45 King, a DJ from the Bronx, where rap began, and a master of the turntables. He had done some work with the Funky Four Plus One More.

Mark and Latifah immediately hit it off. Before long, she started hanging out with some of his hip-hop buddies. They met after school in his basement near the corner of Madison and Stuyvesant Avenues in Irvington, New Jersey's rap central. Everybody was writing rhymes and trying them out over Mark's mixes. At first, Latifah just watched and listened. But Ramsey started pestering her to get in there and try it, too. "Come on, Dana, you know you can rock this jam," he told her. So one day, she grabbed the mic and freestyled. The first time, Latifah didn't sound that great, but she knew she had it in her. She could hear in her head the way she wanted to sound. She just had to figure out how to get it to come out of her mouth.

Mark's basement was always jumping with people from the neighborhood, and eventually they became a posse. Latifah was the only female MC in the group, and she was also the youngest. She called herself Princess of the Posse. Together, the posse formed a group that later became the Flavor Unit. In Mark's basement, Latifah could lose herself. Time seemed to stand still, and all that existed was the music. Some of the greatest teachers graced that small cellar studio. Latifah picked up on all kinds of rhyme, voice, and style. They studied every rap album and every hip-hop magazine (although there were only two of them—*Right On*! and *Word Up*). *Word Up* printed the latest news on who was releasing a record, and *Right On!* gave them the lowdown on any new gossip.

Ramsey was a dreamer. While the rest of the posse practiced their music, Ramsey filled their heads with grand ideas of record deals and lots of money. He predicted they would all make it big and buy houses in the upscale New Jersey neighborhoods of Livingston and Short Hills. In their spare time, they would build nice homes in the 'hood and fix up the parks. At the time, none of them were even thinking about such things. Their goal wasn't to get a record deal. It was to become good. Latifah had plans to go to college to be a newscaster or a lawyer. She liked the idea of arguing a case in court, trying to convince a jury that her side was right. Making a record seemed like far-fetched, crazy talk. "Yeah, yeah, Ramsey, riiight!" they teased him. Ramsey's vision, however, turned out to be more real than any of them would have ever imagined.

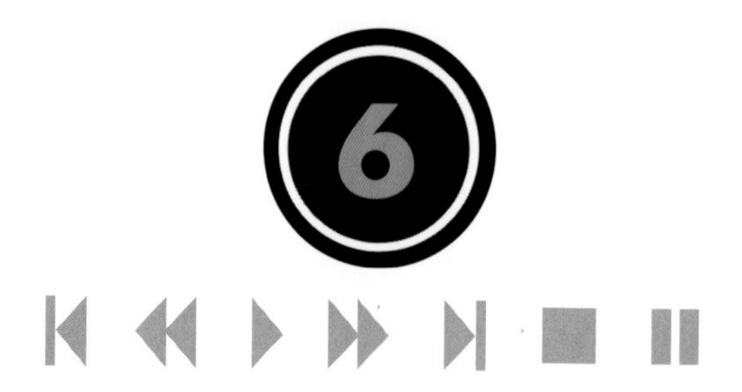

The Queen

Latifah was at the Latin Quarters when Salt-N-Pepa took the stage for the first time in 1987. This female hip-hop group had put out a couple of hits, and their song "My Mic Sounds Nice" was blowing up the charts. Latifah had never seen a female group get up and do their thing before. With their spandex pants, thigh-high boots, and big hair, these girls looked so much different than the male rappers. Latifah had dabbled in rap, but they were different from her, too. She was into casual clothes and sneakers, not glitz and glam.

Not long after, Latifah saw Sweet T and Jazzy Joyce perform. These rappers were regular gals in Adidas sweats and hair pulled back in ponytails. They were straight-up hip-hop. Sweet T even had a fisherman's hat like Latifah's. They were the first women to really rock the Latin Quarters. Jazzy Joyce was one of the best DJs around, and Sweet T ruled the mic with her killer lyrics. After their performance, they left the club in such an uproar that they had to come back and perform the next night. The crowds couldn't get enough. Latifah couldn't get enough.

For the first time, Latifah saw someone who looked and dressed like her, doing something that she had only imagined in her sweetest dreams. Suddenly, it occurred to her that *she* could be up there, rocking the house. Those distant visions began to take form. She could see herself doing it. She could hear Sweet T and Jazzy Joyce chanting with the crowd, "Go La-ti-fah, go, La, go! Give it to 'em, La!"

Up until this point, Latifah wasn't thinking about a record deal. She was content just to do her music in Mark's basement, as a hobby. She had enrolled at Borough of Manhattan Community College, where she was studying broadcast journalism. After the first semester, she sat down with her mother and spoke what seemed to her the craziest words in the world. She wanted to go into the rap game. Surprisingly, Rita told her to go for it. Latifah then convinced the Flavor Unit to hit the stage.

ON THE RADIO

The Flavor Unit was made up of Latee, Apache, Lakim, Chill Rob G, Lord Alibaski, Shakim, Paul, Ramsey, and Latifah—the Princess of the Posse. In the mid 1980s, New Jersey wasn't really on the rap scene. A person could walk into a club and hear the MC shout, "Is Uptown [uptown New York] in the house?" and there would be screams. "Is the Bronx in the house?" and the crowd would yell, "Yeeeeaaaaah!" Next, "Is Brooklyn in the house?" and the place would go wild with hooting and hollering. Brooklyn was always the *in* place to be from. But if the DJ called out, "Is Jersey in the house?" the club would go dead. Every once in a while, some brave partiers would push out a weak "Yeah!" When Latifah started going to the Latin Quarters

One of the first female hip-hop groups to achieve stardom, Salt 'N' Pepa wowed crowds at clubs like the Latin Quarters in New York City. Latifah saw the group perform and realized that she too could own the stage like the trio. Salt 'N' Pepa revived their career in the late '90s and released the 1997 album *Brand New.*

and other clubs, nobody wanted to admit they were from New Jersey. But after a few times performing on stage, the Flavor Unit finally put New Jersey on the rap map.

Record labels soon began to take notice of the Flavor Unit. Latee was the first one to sign a record deal, with Wild Pitch, one of the independent labels emerging in the rap game. It was a huge deal for the Flavor Unit. Now, the rest of them knew someone on the inside. Latee blew the crowds away with his song "This Cut's Got Flavor." The rest of the group were all there when he performed it at the Latin Quarters and rocked the stage. Latifah watched him from the crowd and could feel the excitement for him. It was like being up there herself. Before they knew it, Chill Rob G also signed a deal with Wild Pitch. Then Apache, who Latifah thought was the best rapper of them all, got signed and started working on a record with a guy from the Bronx. Soon, their music was being played on the radio.

Ramsey's vision was unfolding for them. Next, it was Latifah's turn. Ramsey gave her his rent money—$700—to cut a demo. DJ Mark the 45 King and Latifah went into Scott's Studio in Orange, New Jersey, a rinky-dink place off Day Street. Latifah started out with a little intro, "Greetings I Bring from La." She got the beat from a Jamaican rapper called Half Pint. She sang the intro and rapped in a Jamaican dialect, which no one was doing back then. From the start, her style was different.

When they finished a couple of hours later, they were all smiles. They knew they had done a good job. The demo became "Wrath of My Madness," and the B-side was "Princess of the Posse." The next day, Mark gave the demo to Fab Five Freddy, who at the time hosted MTV's *Yo! MTV Raps.* Fab Five Freddy took a copy to Tommy Boy Records. A few days later, Latifah got a call from Monica Lynch, president of Tommy Boy, who was head of artist development at the time. She wanted to meet Latifah to discuss a deal. Just six months earlier, she had gotten her high school diploma. Now, she was working on a record deal.

She hung up the phone and ran into Winki's room, where he was napping. "I'm getting a record deal!" she screamed at the top of her lungs and dove onto the bed. Then she called Ramsey. Latifah felt like she owed so much to her best friend. He had more confidence in her than she ever had in herself. In her vision for the future, she saw herself in college, becoming a newscaster or maybe a lawyer. Ramsey saw fame and fortune. Without his encouragement, and rent money, Latifah might not have made it to this point in her life.

During the summer of 1987, Latifah was sitting in the kitchen of their apartment. By this time, the family had again moved to an apartment above the Modern Era Barber Shop on the corner of Halsted and Elmwood Avenues in East Orange. She was just "chilling," flipping the radio channels between WBLS (107.5 FM) and WRKS-Kiss (98.7 FM). DJ Red Alert on BLS and Marley Marl on Kiss had one of the best over-the-air music battles going that summer. Latifah never knew which one to listen to. If she listened to Kiss, the next day, her friends would tell her what she had missed on BLS. The shows were so good, she often taped them.

Suddenly, she heard a familiar beat. It was the beginning of "Princess of the Posse."

Base lines affect me
My rhymes direct me
Forgive the crowds, oh Lord
They know not why
They sweat me.

Her record—her song—was playing on the radio. Their apartment had windows on both the Halsted and Elmwood sides. Latifah jumped up and ran from window to window, yelling into the streets, "My record is on the radio! My record is on the radio!" She hadn't even officially signed with a label, and yet her song was being played over the airwaves. So excited at the time, she later couldn't even remember if it was Marley Marl or Red Alert who played it. She was the last one of her

After Latifah cut her first demo, "Wrath of My Madness" with the B-side "Princess of the Posse," her friend DJ Mark the 45 King gave it to Fab Five Freddy, host of the popular MTV show *Yo! MTV Raps.* Fab Five Freddy *(above)* began his career as a graffiti artist, and broadened public knowledge of rap in the late '70s and early '80s.

friends to get signed. But she came out blazing. Rock on the Net quotes the *CMJ New Music Report* as warning, "Male rappers step off, because the Queen has arrived."

PROFESSIONALLY KNOWN AS

A decade after she chose her Muslim name, Latifah was selecting yet another name. When it came time to sign her contract with Tommy Boy Records in 1988, her lawyer asked her what her "p.k.a."—or professionally known as—name would be. Up until this time, when she rapped, she called herself "Princess of the Posse" because she was the only girl in her clique. She thought about going with "MC Latifah" or "Latifah the MC." She even considered just leaving it as Latifah, but that seemed too plain.

About this time, the conflict in South Africa against apartheid was coming to a head. Anti-apartheid leader Nelson Mandela was imprisoned, and the United States was pressuring companies to stop doing business with South Africa until the country ended its racist regime. Rita and Latifah would delve into deep conversations about how segregation and racism were alive in America, the very country that opposed apartheid in a nation halfway around the world. They talked about how much they respected women of Africa, whom Latifah believed descended from the most noble royalty of all time. Before the queens of England, there were African queens like Nefertiti and Numidia. Not only did they have extraordinary beauty and power, they had the strength and ability to build up great civilizations. These women were Latifah's foremothers, and she wanted to pay homage to them.

After thinking about it, she decided she wanted to call herself Queen Latifah. When she said it out loud, it made her feel proud. "A queen is a queen when riding high, and when clouded in disgrace, shame, or sorrow, she has dignity," Latifah later wrote. "Being a queen has very little to do with exterior things. It is a state of mind."

When she told her mother, Rita rolled her eyes. "Queen what?" she said. She couldn't see Latifah as a queen yet; maybe

Queen Latifah wanted to display a unique style on the cover of her first album *All Hail the Queen.* Instead of dressing like many other hip-hop stars in baggy pants and gold jewelry, Latifah exhibited the traditional dress of her African heritage. She wears a similar ensemble at the 1990 MTV Video Music Awards (above), where she presented an award with Public Enemy's Flavor Flav.

a princess, but definitely not a queen. In time, however, she got used to it. Latifah later reflected, "In many ways, she was the queen who gave me the guts and the confidence to become one myself. She gave birth, physically and spiritually, to Queen Latifah."

After she signed with Tommy Boy, the label gave her some money to go out and buy an outfit for her cover photos. At the time, Latifah didn't have a manager, so she was on her own to figure out her image. One thing she knew, she did not want to look like every other rapper. The sweat suits, the big gold rope chains—that stuff wasn't her. She thought about who she was—about who Queen Latifah was. She was delicate and kind, and a queen like the women of Africa. She went to an African fabric store on Halsey Street in downtown Newark and picked out a print top. When she couldn't put an outfit together with what they had at the store, she decided to create her own. She asked the woman who ran the store if she would make her a pair of pants to match the top she had picked out. For the photo shoot, she posed in this funky outfit, with a queenlike, turban hat on her head. Unable to find shoes that matched, she went barefoot. People went crazy when they saw the pictures. There certainly was no rapper like her. Later, while on tour, she wore the same outfit—which saved her a lot of money—with no shoes. The crowds went wild. The Jungle Brothers, who were on tour with her, nicknamed her Mama Zulu because of her African duds.

Latifah's first album, *All Hail the Queen*, was released in 1989. She was 18 years old. Her debut album sold well, climbing to the top ten on the R&B charts. In 1991, she released a second album, *Nature of a Sista'*. Latifah's sophomore album was not quite as popular as *All Hail the Queen*. Even though that is a common phenomenon, when the contract with Tommy Boy was up, the label decided not to re-sign her. She tried to stay positive and focus on her good fortune so far, but things were about to get much worse before they would get better.

Losing Winki

Although her second album wasn't as popular as her first, the single "Latifah's Had It Up 2 Here," soared to the top ten. She was nominated for a Grammy award for Best Rap Solo Performance in *All Hail the Queen*, and she performed a concert tour in Europe. She even landed a small part in Spike Lee's movie *Jungle Fever.* Life was still pretty good for the twenty-two-year-old rapper.

Ramsey and Latifah shared an apartment in the Dixon Mills complex in Jersey City. Latee had just gotten his own place nearby, and some of the old gang got together to help him move. One of the last pieces of furniture was an enormous and heavy couch, which had to be hauled up the steps and crammed through the doorway. They had to stretch, strain,

Though Queen Latifah began achieving stardom in her early twenties, she maintained close ties to her family and home state of New Jersey. Here, the rising star poses in front of a neighborhood shop displaying her poster in its window.

angle, and maneuver to get the monstrosity inside. When they finally managed to get it into the apartment, an hour later, they all collapsed on the floor, exhausted.

As they relaxed, Latifah got a page, a 911 from Ramsey, who was working at a video store a few blocks from Latee's new place. She called Ramsey at once, but before she could even get out "hello", he interrupted her. "Your brother had an accident on his motorcycle," Ramsey said. Latifah asked if it was serious. "I think so," Ramsey replied. Latifah's heart dropped, and her mind went numb.

Latifah hurried to University Hospital in Newark, where Winki had been taken. Along the way, it started to rain. It had been warm and sunny all weekend, but it suddenly turned dark and stormy. Latifah told herself Winki would be fine. He had become a police officer, and he was both highly trained and tough.

But on the drive, Latifah was hit with a strange and horrible feeling, as if she wasn't herself anymore. The feeling frightened her because, ever since they were kids, Latifah believed she and her brother had a spiritual connection. They were both Pisces—two fish swimming up and down the same stream. As the rain began falling harder, Latifah got a chill, and her whole body shook.

Outside the emergency entrance, a tow truck held Winki's mangled bike. "Oh, God," Latifah prayed. "Please let him be all right. Please, God, please!" When she got to the emergency waiting room, Winki's friends were all standing around. "Where's my brother?" Latifah demanded. They led her to a family waiting room, where her mother sat in a brown chair. She looked eerily calm. Latifah collapsed in the chair next to her. Rita picked up Latifah's hand and spoke in a soft, slow voice, "Dana, Winki's been in an accident. He was hit by a car. His bike went under the car. All we can do right now is pray."

They waited what seemed like an eternity. Finally, a doctor walked into the room, wearing surgical scrubs. Her expression was strained, like she had something painful to say. "I'm sorry, but we lost him," she said.

For a moment, Latifah stared up in shock and disbelief. "No, he's not dead," she screamed. "You better go back in that room and do something! Go back in there!"

"We cracked his chest and tried to pump his heart manually," the doctor answered. "We used eight more pints of blood than we would on anyone else. We knew he was a police officer. We did everything. But his injuries were too severe, and we couldn't save him. I'm sorry."

Latifah had bought Winki that motorcycle, a Kawasaki Ninja ZX7, for his twenty-fourth birthday. Earlier, she had bought a

Honda CBR600 for herself, and Winki thought it was so "fly" that he wanted one, too. So Latifah picked the phattest, baddest bike around for him. They would take their bikes out on the road, just the two of them, where no one could bother them, where they could be a team. She never imagined that bike, bought out of love, would cause Winki's death. "Losing Winki was like losing half of myself," she said. "I was numb and empty."

Just a month ago, they had started putting the finishing touches on a new family home. The house had been Latifah's dream. Once her career took off, she rarely got to see her family. She had moved in with her dancers, Kika and Al, in Co-Op City in the Bronx. They had a fun bachelorette pad, but something was missing. She missed family dinners, renting movies with Winki and her mom, waking up in the morning and having breakfast with them. She wanted to be under the same roof with her family again. So she decided to buy a house big enough for all of them to live. She found an unfinished house in Wayne, New Jersey. At the time, it was just a shell. But that was perfect for Latifah. She could create a design that had zones—where everyone could have their own space. Her mother would get the master bedroom, of course. And Winki would get the basement.

One night, after they closed on the house, Winki and Latifah drove by the place. They didn't have the keys yet, but they wanted to check it out. They crawled in one of the windows, and they peeked around the house, led by Winki's police flashlight. They imagined how it would look when it was all decorated. Latifah had picked out a leather bedroom set from a fancy store on Madison Avenue in New York for Winki. She bought her mom an elegant burlwood set that she had her eyes on for two years in Beverly Hills, California. For her room, she was having a cherry-wood bedroom set custom built. The next day, they came back, just when the workmen were installing the black Jacuzzi. Winki climbed into it with his clothes on and kicked back. Latifah remembered how silly he looked.

Queen Latifah claims that her father instilled within his children "a need for speed." Soon after she bought her Honda CBR600 motorcycle, Queen Latifah's brother, Winki, declared his desire for one. Latifah bought him a different model for his 24th birthday. Tragically, Winki crashed his cycle into another vehicle and sustained fatal injuries.

Latifah couldn't wait to move in. She envisioned a house full of activity, laughter, and peace. Not more than a month later, Winki was gone, and Latifah's dreams were shattered.

GETTING THROUGH IT

For months after Winki's death, Latifah was a mess. She went through the motions of her daily life—waking, showering, and eating—like a zombie. She just couldn't get past the pain. She felt a gaping hole inside of her, a huge void. Gradually, she pulled herself away from reality, turning to drugs and alcohol

LATIFAH'S LAWS: BE FREE FROM ADDICTION

"By the time this book is in your hands, I should be free from my addiction. My habit is cigarettes.

"Being addicted to something, to anything, takes away your power. Here's what I mean: I hate smoking. I know that it's unhealthy. I hate the way it makes my body feel, the way it makes my clothes smell. It makes *me* smell. But I still want my smokes. I need them, and that need is beyond my control. I hate having something control me like that.

"One of my proudest moments in my life was when I quit smoking after my brother died. I wanted to cleanse myself. I spent so much time filling my body with alcohol, with weed, and with cigarettes that I couldn't feel a thing. Suddenly, I was terrified. Nothing was coming in—not pain, not pleasure.

"I quit cold turkey. I encouraged myself with Post-it notes stuck up all over the house: YOU CAN DO IT, DANA! DON'T EVEN THINK ABOUT PICKING UP A CIGARETTE. COME ON GIRL, JUST ONE MORE DAY. I knew it was one day at a time and that each

to mask the hurt. She started smoking marijuana and drinking booze every day.

Latifah quickly fell into a routine that took her in a downward spiral. Each morning, she woke up crying, even before she opened her eyes. She'd force herself to stop and light a joint. As soon as she was high, she'd slip on a pair of blue-tinted sunglasses. Then she drove to East Orange to see if her mother needed her. After visiting Rita, she went to the park and shot hoops. All afternoon, she threw shots and listened to the ball echoing off the concrete. But none of it erased Winki from her

day I didn't smoke was one day closer to quitting altogether. And I did it. It took a while for my body to adjust to not getting the nicotine it craved, but eventually, I started to feel great. My senses became alive again. I could smell more keenly and distinguish subtle tastes. My lips began to tingle. I could work out longer and breathe easier. I never realized how much abuse my body was taking from those cigarettes. I vowed I would never pick up another butt. And then I lapsed. . . .

"I'm working hard to quit again. . . . I have to do it if I want to be free. I have to regain control. . . . If you see me on the streets with a cigarette, step to me. Because if there's one thing that people with an addiction need, it's accountability. If you hold me accountable (without being rude about it), like it or not, it will help me. . . . I will realize that people have their eye on me . . . I don't want to let them down. And even more, I don't want to let myself down. It helps to know that people are out there rooting for you when you are in a rough game."

mind. On the way home, she stopped off at the liquor store. Then she spent the rest of the night smoking marijuana and drinking until she passed out.

Every day, she reached for the blue shades. They hid her red eyes, her pain. They shielded her from reality. But she knew her false escape wasn't helping her—or her mother. She decided to talk to the only other person who could understand what she was going through: her aunt Elaine. Elaine had lost more than one brother, and yet she seemed to have her life on track. Latifah asked her, "How do you get over something like this?"

Elaine gave her a bit of straightforward advice. "You don't ever get over something like this," she said. "You get through it." All the while, Latifah had been trying to make the pain go away instead of learning to deal with it. "Losing a loved one is like being an amputee," Latifah later explained. "When you lose a limb, you still feel it, even though it's not there. It itches and it hurts. I can still feel Winki. It was helpful to think about him as if he were still here."

Latifah knew it was time to get on with her life. Projects kept coming her way, and movie offers were rolling in. Soon, she landed a starring role on *Living Single*, a FOX sitcom, for which she also wrote and performed the theme music. She left New Jersey to start shooting in Los Angeles. Since Winki's death, Rita and Latifah had been clinging to each other. Latifah worried about being so far away from her mother. She called home every night.

One night, shortly after she arrived in L.A., Latifah slipped Winki's bike key on a gold chain and hung it around her neck. Then she got on her bike. She desperately wanted one more ride with her big brother. She hadn't ridden a motorcycle since Winki died. Although she was still afraid of the loneliness and pain, she decided it was time to face her fears. She fired up the bike and took off onto Ventura Highway. It was 2:00 in the morning, and she felt free out there on the road by herself. "Let's ride, Winki," she screamed. "Let's ride!"

After Winki's death, Latifah turned to drugs and alcohol for solace. She realized, however, that her actions were self-destructive, and that she still had a lot of living to do. More projects came her way, including a lead role in the FOX hit show *Living Single*, co-starring *(from left)* Erika Alexander, Kim Fields, and Kim Coles.

BLACK REIGN

Before Winki's accident, Latifah had signed a record contract with Motown. Exhausted from the ordeal, she worried she didn't have an album in her. When Winki died, the songs in her died, too. She began talking to Winki, hoping it would give her the strength she needed. Being around the music and listening to the songs she and Winki loved helped carry her over the rough spots. She poured her pain into something creative. The last cut on her album *Black Reign* was "Winki's Theme." It was more personal than anything she had ever done. By this time, she had overcome the weed and the monotonous afternoons at the basketball park. She found another way to express her emotions. "Winki's Theme" was the first song in which she actually sang. A mixture of jazz, reggae, rap, and instruments, the song opened up her soul.

Out on tour, some in the audience knew the meaning behind "Winki's Theme." They understood why she'd fall into tears as she sang it. Often, she looked out into the crowd and see a lot of fans in tears, too.

> This jam is dedicated to my brother Winki
> Who is looking down on me from heaven
> Watching my every move as usual."

Latifah felt that *Black Reign* was as much Winki's album as it was hers. She called him a coproducer because he was with her every step of the way. The hit single "U.N.I.T.Y." off the album won a Grammy award.

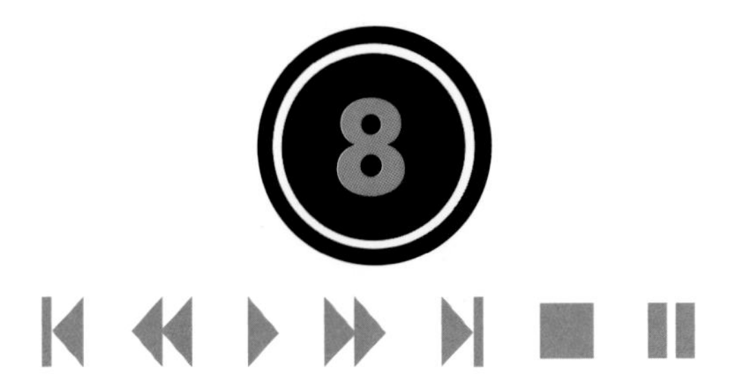

Dividing Eggs

After releasing her fourth rap album, *Order in the Court*, in 1998, Latifah shifted much of her energy to acting. "I never pictured myself as just a rapper," she said in a 2006 interview for beliefnet.com. "I always wanted to act and do whatever else I could do." Latifah believed that unless she could call herself the best rapper on the planet, she wouldn't "put all of her eggs in one basket." Instead, she kept her eyes and her mind open for other opportunities. Clearly, people loved to watch her strut her stuff on stage. Hollywood wanted to find out if she could rock it in front of a movie camera as well.

She made her film debut in Spike Lee's critically acclaimed *Jungle Fever* in 1991 and followed it with other supporting

Queen Latifah's first starring movie role was in *Set It Off,* in which she plays expert car thief and bank robber Cleo Sims. Latifah's portrayal of the lesbian character was so convincing that false rumors began circulating that Latifah herself is gay. Latifah advocates gay rights and has been involved with gay and lesbian human rights campaigns.

actress parts in movies like *House Party 2* and *Juice*. During the mid-1990s, Latifah's major roles were in tough, gangster pictures. She broke through to center spotlight with her own TV sitcom, *Living Single*, which aired from 1993 to 1998 on FOX.

But Latifah first attracted wide media attention for her role in the 1996 box-office hit *Set It Off*, for which she also performed some of the music. This gangster picture is about four friends from Los Angeles who plan and execute a bank robbery. They all have differing motives for the heist, even though they all want better opportunities than are available to them. In the movie, Latifah plays Cleo Sims, a lesbian expert car thief.

Her portrayal of a lesbian set off wild rumors about her personal life. In her autobiography, Latifah admits that Cleo was one of her most challenging parts, and one of which she is extremely proud. She worked the role of a hard-core, from-the-'hood lesbian and played it to a tee. She did so well as the character, people wanted to know how much of Cleo was in Latifah.

Aside from the ridiculous implication that there is no difference between fact and fiction and that the public believes everything it sees, Latifah found the media's questions insulting. "A woman cannot be strong, outspoken, competent at running her own business, handle herself physically, play a very convincing role in a move, know what she wants—and go for it—without being gay?" Latifah commented. "Come on." She was proud to have been so thoroughly convincing in her role that people believed she was her character, but she resented the assumptions made by the public.

Although not a lesbian, Latifah is an advocate for gay rights issues. In 2000, she joined Melissa Etheridge, Garth Brooks, George Michael, the Pet Shop Boys, and k.d. lang in Washington, D.C., to perform at the Equality Rocks benefit concert in support of a gay and lesbian human-rights campaign.

Nominated for a Best Supporting Actress Academy Award for her role as Matron "Mama" Morton in the 2002 smash movie hit of the Broadway musical *Chicago*, Queen Latifah arrives to the 75th annual Academy Awards.

After being cast in the plum role of Matron "Mama" Morton in the movie of the Broadway musical *Chicago* in 2002, Latifah finally gained mainstream acting success. For her role in this film, which was a box office success and won the Oscar for Best Picture, Latifah received an Academy Award nomination for Best Supporting Actress. *Chicago* changed Latifah's life in many ways. "Man, they should've spelled it *Chicag000*, with a buncha extra zeros at the end," Latifah told Roger Moore in a January 2006 interview for the *Star Online*.

The week the Oscar nominations were announced in 2003, *Bringing Down the House*, in which Latifah costarred with comedy legends Steve Martin and Eugene Levy, was number one at the box office. "I showed people I could do some different sorts of things," Latifah told Moore, "that I could handle different types of music, and that I was commercial, all in, like the same week!"

Bringing Down the House was one of Latifah's biggest film roles. In the film, Peter Sanderson, played by Steve Martin, is a lonely, divorced, straight-laced attorney who is still in love with his ex-wife and doesn't understand why she left him. Ready to move on, he begins chatting with a brainy blonde bombshell on the Internet. When she shows up for their first face-to-face encounter, he finds out she isn't who she said she was. Instead, it's Charlene (Latifah), a convict who has escaped from prison but claims she's innocent and wants Peter to help clear her name. When Peter wants nothing to do with her, Charlene turns his life upside down, jeopardizing his chances to get back together with his wife and land a billion-dollar client. Racial undertones play a large part of the film's humor, but Latifah had fun with it.

Some critics found *Bringing Down the House* offensive, which Latifah predicted. "There's always that possibility," she told Wilson Morales in a March 2003 BlackFilm.com interview. "You can't please everyone all the time. We are willing to take a chance with it. We think it's a comedy and it's meant

Queen Latifah poses with costars Steve Martin and Linus for press photos at the Hollywood premiere of their hit movie *Bringing Down the House.* In her 20-year career, Latifah has enjoyed huge success as a music, TV, and movie star and has worked with legends like Martin, Emma Thompson, and John Travolta.

to be laughed at and not taken too seriously anyway." At the same time, Latifah admitted that there were some jokes in the original script that she wouldn't do, and they were cut from the film.

Her next movie project was *Taxi*, a comedy remake of a French film of the same name. She costarred with comedian Jimmy Fallon, who plays Andy Washburn, a bumbling New York cop who can do everything but drive. Latifah is speed-demon cabbie Elle Williams, who cruises the streets of New York in her tricked-out taxi. Elle has earned the reputation of New York's fastest cabbie. But being a cab driver is only a pit stop on the road of Elle's ultimate dream: race car champion. Desperate to earn respect from his department, Andy convinces Elle to team up with him in a mission to catch a band of Brazilian bank robbers.

Latifah chose this movie for several reasons. Aside from the fact that both her dad and brother were policemen, she felt a close connection to her character, Elle Williams, who dreams of racing cars. An avid NASCAR fan, Latifah has loved racing ever since she was a little girl. When she was about five years old, her father took her and Winki out on Highway 78 in New Jersey before it opened. He flew down the deserted highway at 125 miles per hour. From that point on, Latifah always felt the need for speed.

The following year, Latifah reprised her role as Gina Norris, the character she played in the 2004 movie *Barbershop 2*, in *Beauty Shop*. In this film, Gina is a long way from the Chicago barbershop, trying to make a name for herself at an exclusive, mostly white salon in Atlanta. But when her flamboyant, arrogant boss (played by Kevin Bacon) hands her one too many insults, she walks out, taking the shampoo girl with her. Gina opens her own salon in the 'hood, where many of her clients follow her.

Like *Bringing Down the House*, *Beauty Shop* is a movie that deals with racial issues. Although Latifah doesn't search out

In 2006 Queen Latifah starred in *The Last Holiday*, a remake of a 1950 film. Latifah's character maintains a conservative lifestyle until she learns she has only weeks to live. She then lets go of her reservations and pursues her wildest dreams. Latifah and co-star LL Cool J, another hip-hop star-turned actor, are pictured in the photograph above.

movies about race, she does feel that America has plenty of racial problems, and she enjoys being in a creative process that confronts them. According to Latifah, the problem with today's society is that no one talks about or deals with the issues anymore. "I miss the '70s where you had shows like *The Jefferson's* and *All in the Family* where black people could be black and white people could be white," she said in a 2005 interview with MovieHole.net. "Racists could be racists, and non-racists could be non-racists, but it was talked about. You could form your own opinion as to how ignorant or how reasonable these people were being." In today's world, she says, "We're just politically correct, and we act as if it went away. It didn't go away."

In 2006, Latifah starred in *The Last Holiday*, a remake of a 1950 movie with the same name. Georgia Byrd (played by Latifah) is a shy, meek, and humble woman who is always bending over backwards for everyone else. In the past, her life has been ruled by fear. She's afraid to spend her money in case she needs it. She won't approach the man she's in love with in fear he might reject her. Instead, she buries all her hopes and dreams in a "Book of Possibilities." When diagnosed with a terminal illness that only gives her three weeks to live, Georgia throws caution to the wind and chooses to live out her dreams and goals.

The Last Holiday had a huge impact on Latifah. Georgia Byrd inspired her to live better, braver, and bolder. "By living in Georgia Byrd's shoes, it made me realize how important life is, how short time is, how important it is to follow your dreams and your goals," Latifah told beliefnet.com. In the original film, the lead character is a man—George Bird. But that didn't make Latifah flinch. In all her roles, she likes to be creative with the characters. Oftentimes, talent drives the script, and the characters have to be adjusted to fit the actors a studio wants. "I never limit myself to supposedly typical female roles, let alone African-American female ones," Latifah explained to BlackNews.com in January 2006.

That year, Latifah joined an impressive ensemble for the black comedy *Stranger Than Fiction*. The movie starred Will Ferrell as an ordinary man who realizes he is a character in a novel, and that the author of the novel will soon kill him off. Like Georgia Byrd, he learns to live life to the fullest in the limited time he has left. Latifah acted opposite esteemed Oscar-winner Emma Thompson, who said Latifah "nailed the part." "We clicked from day one," Latifah told the press. Working with such strong, seasoned performers has helped Latifah grow as an actress.

Additionally, Latifah starred in the important HBO movie *Life Support,* a true story of an AIDS activist. She also completed filming a lead role for the movie version of the stage musical *Hairspray.*

Currently, she is working on a remake of the 1984 movie *All of Me,* in which she will both star and executive produce. In the '80s version of this wacky comedy, the soul of a dying heiress jumps into the body of her lawyer. The new millennium film will have a slightly different twist. This time around, the Queen plays a liberal stuck in the body of a conservative. It may turn out to be her funniest role yet. Latifah is also filming *Mad Money*—a movie about three female employees of the Federal Reserve who plot to steal money that is about to be destroyed. The movie, which includes A-list costars Diane Keaton and Katie Holmes, is due out in 2008.

FLAVOR UNIT AND MORE

For some, being a hip-hop queen and a movie star is enough. But Latifah was born to spread her wings much wider.

When she first started touring and doing club dates around the country, she had no clue about money. She didn't yet know when she should get paid and how to make sure she got her share. Common sense told her that she shouldn't collect the money herself. So with each show, she sent a different person to track down the promoters. At most shows, this person is called the road manager. But Latifah didn't have one yet. As far as she was concerned, she was still just a girl rapping out of someone's basement.

One night, after a show in Connecticut, Latifah sent one of her cousins to pick up her money from the promoter. The promoter spun a story about there not being as many people in the audience as he thought. All he had for Latifah was $3,000, not the $5,000 she was owed. Latifah's cut was not dependent

Thanks to her achievements in movies, television, and music, Queen Latifah received a star on the Hollywood Walk of Fame in January 2006. Though she has accomplished much and inspired many, Queen Latifah would no doubt be the first to say that she has much more to do, see, say, and achieve.

on how many tickets were sold. The deal was $5,000, sellout or no sellout. When her cousin returned with the news, Shakim, one of her friends from the Flavor Unit, offered to go get her money—all of it.

Latifah never heard what Shakim said to the promoter, but ten minutes later he returned with every penny. Latifah quickly realized that Shakim could take care of business. Not long after, she asked him to be her manager. In time, Shakim wasn't content just being road manager. He wanted to do it all. So Shakim, Rita, and Latifah learned the business together. While Latifah and Shakim were on the road, Rita took care of things at home, taking phone calls and handling correspondence. Within a few years, Latifah's record deals and regular gigs grew into an entrepreneurial business—Flavor Unit Entertainment. Soon, they began managing other groups, too. Today, Flavor Unit Entertainment represents acts such as Naughty by Nature and LL Cool J.

In addition to her music enterprise, Latifah is a celebrity spokesperson for Cover Girl cosmetics and Curvation ladies underwear and clothing line. She also voices commercials for Pizza Hut. From 1999 to 2001, she even hosted her own talk show, *The Queen Latifah Show.* Recently, she has added the title of Hollywood producer to her list of skills. She has worked as a producer on films such as *Beauty Shop*, *The Cookout*, and *Bringing Down the House.*

Even with her booming acting career, Latifah still hasn't forgotten about her first love—music. In 2002, she released a greatest-hits CD titled *She's the Queen: A Collection of Hits.* In 2004, she switched gears and recorded a soul and jazz album called *The Dana Owens Album.* Many films, both those she has appeared in and others, feature her music.

With so much accomplished, it is hard to believe there are any mountains left for Latifah to climb. However, she believes that as long as she is alive, there's much more to learn and do.

She feels like she has a lot of growing to do personally, spiritually, mentally, and emotionally. Meanwhile, she will keep looking for more opportunities—dividing those eggs between the baskets. As she tells it, "So, I guess I'll be hanging around till God says, 'You're good, come on back.'"

APPENDIX

DISCOGRAPHY

The Dana Owens Collection, 2004
She's the Queen: A Collection of Hits, 2002
Order in the Court, 1998
Black Reign, 1993
Nature of a Sista', 1991
All Hail the Queen, 1989

FILMOGRAPHY

Hairspray (2007)—Motormouth Maybelle
Life Support (2007)—Ana Willis
Perfect Christmas (2007)—Narrator
Stranger than Fiction (2006)—Penny Escher
Ice Age 2: The Meltdown (2006) (voice)—Ellie
Ice Age: The Meltdown (2006) (voice)—Ellie
Last Holiday (2006)—Georgia Byrd
The Muppets' Wizard of Oz (2005)—Auntie Em
Beauty Shop (2005)—Gina Norris
Taxi (2004)—Elle
The Cookout (2004)—Security Guard
The Fairly Odd Parents, "Crash Nebula" (2004) (voice)—
Pam Dromeda
Sister, Sister (2004) episode—Simone

Barbershop 2: Back in Business (2004)—Gina
Scary Movie 3 (2003)—Aunt Shaneequa
Bringing Down the House (2003)—Charlene Morton
Kung Faux (2003) series—voiceover/various
Chicago (2002)—Matron "Mama" Morton
Pinocchio (2002) (voice)
Brown Sugar (2002)—Francine
The Country Bears (2002)—Cha-Cha
Living with the Dead (2002)—Midge Harmon
Platinum Comedy Series: Roasting Shaquille O'Neal (2002)
Spin City
- "Sleeping with the Enemy" (2001)—Robin Jones
- "Yeah Baby!" (2001)—Robin Jones

Bringing Out the Dead (1999) (voice)—Dispatcher Love
The Bone Collector (1999)—Thelma
Mama Flora's Family (1998)—Diana
Living Out Loud (1998)—Liz Bailey
Sphere (1998)—Alice "Teeny" Fletcher
Living Single (1993–1998)—Khadijah Jame
Hoodlum (1997)—Sulie
Mad TV, "Episode #2.13" (1997) TV episode—host
Set It Off (1996)—Cleopatra "Cleo" Sims
My Life (1993)—Theresa
Sisters in the Name of Rap (1992)
Juice (1992)—Ruffhouse M.C.

The Fresh Prince of Bel-Air
- "She Ain't Heavy" (1991)—Dee Dee
- "Working It Out" (1991)—Marissa Redman

House Party 2 (1991)—Zora
Jungle Fever (1991)—Lashawn
In Living Color, "Episode #2.1" (1990)—musical guest

SOUNDTRACKS

Last Holiday (2006) (performer: "Every Time I Feel the Spirit," "Farther Along")
Barbershop 2: Back in Business (2004) (performer: "SportsCenter Theme," "Wade in the Water")
The 75th Annual Academy Awards (2003) (performer: "I Move On")
Bringing Down the House (2003) (writer and producer: "Do Your Thing")
Chicago (2002) (performer: "When You're Good to Mama" [1975], "Class" [1975])
Brown Sugar (2002) (writer: "The Unit")
What's the Worst That Could Happen? (2001) (performer: "Everywhere You Go")
Living Out Loud (1998) (performer: "Lush Life," "Goin' Out of My Head," "Be Anything (But Be Mine)")
The Associate (1996) (writer and performer: "Mr. Big Stuff")

Girls Town (1996) (performer: "U.N.I.T.Y.")
The Walking Dead (1995) ("Conflict")
White Men Can't Jump (1992) (writer and perfomer: "The Hook")
New Jack City (1991) ("For the Love of Money," "Living for the City")

PRODUCER

Life Support (2007) (executive producer)
Perfect Christmas (2007) (producer)
Beauty Shop (2005) (producer)
The Cookout (2004) (producer)
Bringing Down the House (2003) (executive producer)
Queen Latifah Show (1999) (executive producer)

WRITER

The Cookout (2004)

CHRONOLOGY

1970 **March 18** Born Dana Elaine Owens in Newark, New Jersey.

1988 Signs a record deal with Tommy Boy Records.

1989 Debut album, *All Hail the Queen*, released, containing her first radio hit "Ladies First," as well as "Dance for Me" and "Wrath of My Madness."

1990 Helps David Bowie on one of his remixes of "Fame 90."

1991 **February** Nominated for a Grammy award for Best Rap Solo Performance on *All Hail the Queen*.

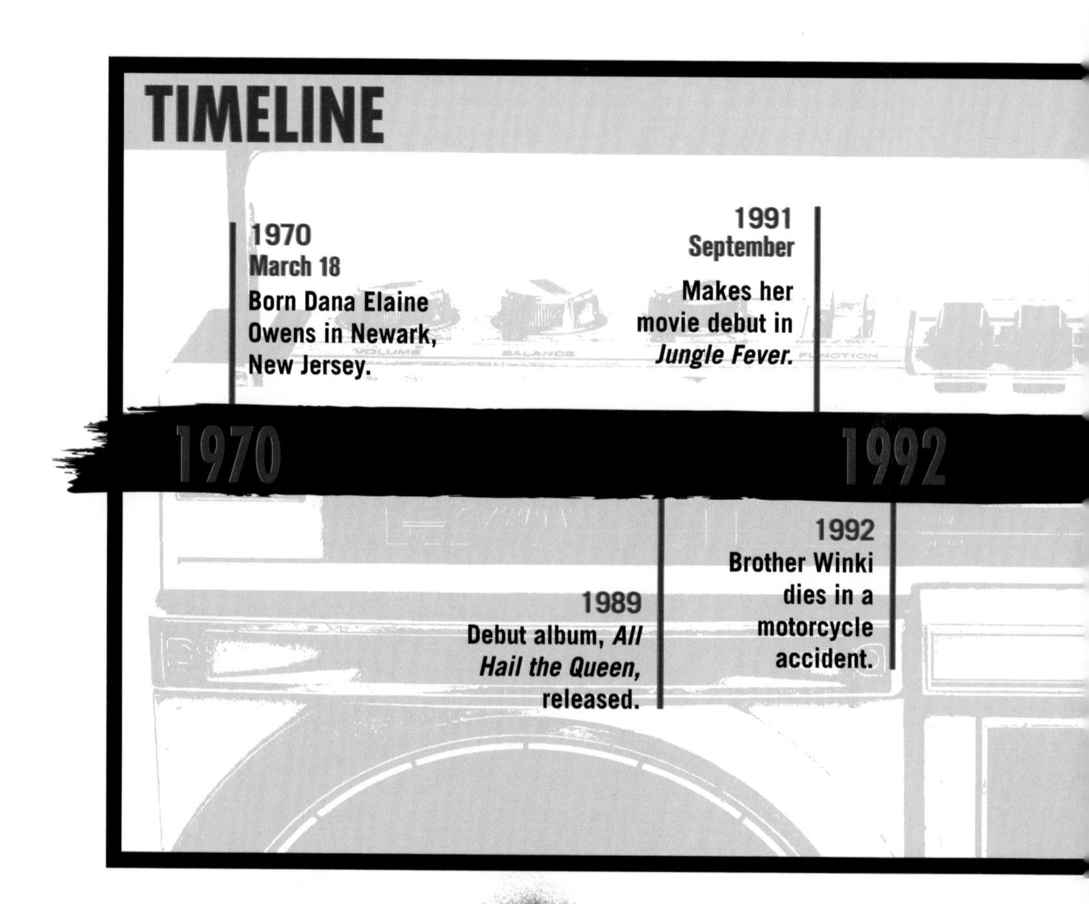

1991 **September** Releases her second album, *Nature of a Sista'*; signs a new contract with Motown Records; makes her movie debut in *Jungle Fever.*

1992 Brother Winki dies in a motorcycle accident.

1993 Releases *Black Reign,* which includes the hit "U.N.I.T.Y."; *Black Reign* is the first album by a female MC to go gold.

1995 Wins a Grammy award for Best Rap Solo Performance for "U.N.I.T.Y."

1996 **February** Arrested for drug and weapons charges after being stopped for speeding in California; marijuana

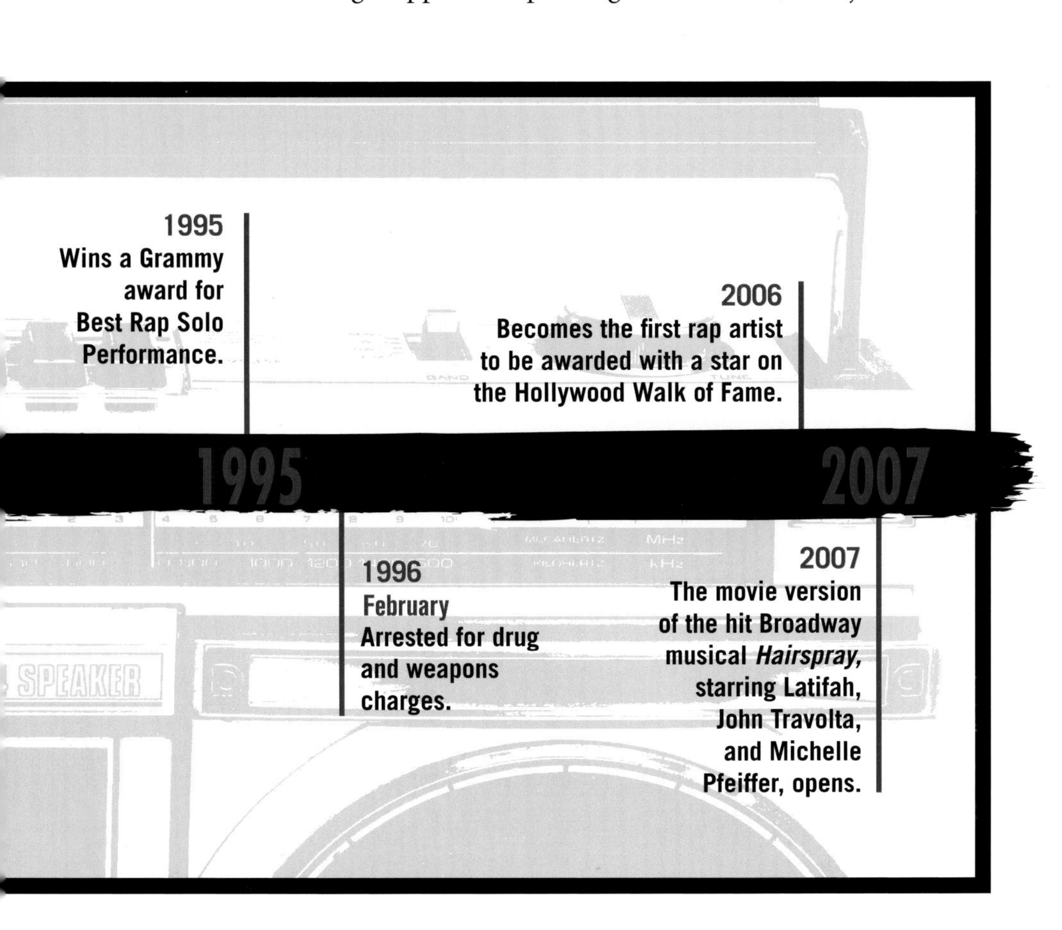

and a loaded gun are found in the vehicle; she pleads guilty and pays a fine.

1996 **September** Appears in the film *Set It Off.*

1997 **January** Rock and Roll Hall of Fame's 500 Songs that Shaped Rock and Roll includes "Ladies First."

1997 **September** Honored with the Aretha Franklin Award for Entertainer of the Year at the 1997 Soul Train Lady of Soul Awards.

1998 **June** Album *Order in the Court* is released.

1998 **December** Named one of the Most Fascinating Women of 1998 by *Ladies Home Journal.*

1999 Nominated for two NAACP Image Awards for Outstanding Supporting Actress in a Motion Picture (*Living Out Loud*) and Outstanding Actress in a Television Movie/Mini-Series/Dramatic Special (*Mama Flora's Family*); VH1's *100 Greatest Women of Rock & Roll* includes Queen Latifah at number 72.

2000 Autobiography *Ladies First: Revelations of a Strong Woman* hits bookstores.

2002 Appears in the film *Brown Sugar*; releases a greatest-hits collection, *She's a Queen: A Collection of Hits.*

2003 For her role in the film *Chicago* she is nominated for a Golden Globe for Best Supporting Actress; is nominated for a Screen Actors Guild award (SAG) for Best Supporting Actress; wins a SAG award as part of Best Cast Performance; and is nominated for an Academy Award for Best Supporting Actress; also, VH1's *50 Greatest Hip-Hop Artists* ranks Queen Latifah at number 24.

2004 Stars in *Barbershop 2: Back in Business* and *Taxi*; releases the *Dana Owens Album*; wins an NAACP Image Award for Outstanding Actress in a Motion Picture for her role in *Bringing Down the House.*

2005 *Beauty Shop* hits the big screen; Queen Latifah wins a Kid's Choice Award for the Wannabe Award, the celebrity kids most want to be like.

2006 Becomes the first rap artist to be awarded with a star on the Hollywood Walk of Fame; *Last Holiday,* with LL Cool J, opens in theaters; Latifah plays the voice of Ellie in the animated film *Ice Age: The Meltdown* and *Ice Age 2.*

2007 The movie version of the hit Broadway musical *Hairspray,* starring Latifah, John Travolta, and Michelle Pfeiffer, opens.

GLOSSARY

alliteration The repeated use of the same sound at the beginning of a phrase; for example, "sloppy slouching is something I won't do," from Queen Latifah's "Ladies First."

assonance The repeated use of the same vowel sound in a phrase; for example, "Who's the mother of a brother who's the brother of another," from Queen Latifah's "Ladies First."

beat The rhythm in a piece of music.

DJ Short for disc jockey. Creates the background music for rap songs by manipulating recordings through such techniques as audio mixing, scratching, and backspinning.

doo-wop A style of rhythm and blues music that became popular in the 1950s; in this type of music, small groups sing strings of words and nonsense sounds over a rhythmic melody.

freestyle A type of rapping in which lyrics are improvised.

gangsta rap A style of rap music associated with street gangs that uses violent, tough-talking lyrics.

MC Stands for master of ceremonies, a performer who introduces other performers to the audience, or who raps on top of a DJ's beats.

mic Another term for microphone.

mixing To blend different sounds or music into one soundtrack.

posse A slang term for a group of friends.

rhyme The verses of a rap song.

sample A portion or section of a whole song.

scratching To rub a record back and forth on a turntable so that the needle makes a scratching sound.

tag Another word for a graffiti mark; a tagger is a graffiti artist, and to paint tags is to paint one's initials.

BIBLIOGRAPHY

Aames, Ethan. "Interview: Queen Latifah on *Taxi*," Cinema Confidential, October 7, 2004. Available online. URL: http://www.cinecon.com/news.php?id=0410071.

Leventry, Ellen. "It Was Just a Gang for God," beliefnet.com, January 12, 2006. Available online. URL: http://www.beliefnet.com/story/182/story_18272_1.html.

Moore, Roger. "Q&A with *Last Holiday* Star Queen Latifah," *Star Online,* January 12, 2006. Available online. URL: http://www.star-ecentral.com.

Morales, Wilson. "Bringing Down the House: An Interview with Queen Latifah," BlackFilm.com, Mar. 7, 2003. Available online. URL: http://blackfilm.com/20030307/features/queenlatifah.shtml.

Morris, Clint. "Interview with Queen Latifah," MovieHole.net, March 31, 2005. Available online. URL: http://www.moviehole.net/news/5354.html.

Queen Latifah, with Karen Hunter. *Ladies First: Revelations of a Strong Woman.* New York: William Morrow and Company, Inc., 1999.

Williams, Kam. "Queen Latifah: *The Last Holiday* Interview," BlackNews.com, January 9, 2006. Available online. URL: http://www.blacknews.com/pr/queenlatifah101.html.

FURTHER READING

BOOKS

Baker, Soren. *The Music Library: The History of Rap and Hip-Hop.* San Diego, Calif.: Lucent Books, 2006.

Bloom, Sarah. *Queen Latifah.* Philadelphia, PA: Chelsea House Publishers, 2002.

Haskins, Jim. *One Nation Under a Groove: Rap Music and Its Roots.* New York: Hyperion, 2000.

Light, Alan (editor). *The Vibe History of Hip Hop.* New York: Three Rivers Press, 1999.

Lommel, Cookie. *The History of Rap Music.* Philadelphia, PA: Chelsea House, 2001.

Ruth, Amy. *Queen Latifah.* Minneapolis, Minn.: Lerner Publications, 2001.

Snyder, Gail. *Queen Latifah.* Philadelphia, PA: Mason Crest Publishers, 2007.

WEB SITES

Queen Latifah's Fan Site

http://www.queenlatifah.info

PHOTO CREDITS

PAGE

12: Associated Press, AP/ Jennifer Graylock
16: AP/Wyatt Counts
17: Associated Press, AP/ TAMMIE ARROYO
21: Index Stock Imagery/Barry Winiker
23: © Getty Images
28: AP Images
33: Associated Press, AP/MIKE DERER
37: © Jason Reed/Reuters/ Corbis
40: Associated Press, AP/ MIKE DERER
42: Associated Press, AP/ JUSTIN SUTCLIFFE
45: © Neal Preston/CORBIS
51: Associated Press, AP
52: © Getty Images
58: © YOUNG RUSSELL/ CORBIS SYGMA
61: Associated Press, AP/ HENNY RAY ABRAMS
63: © Getty Images
66: © diverseimages/Getty Images
69: © diverseimages/Getty Images
73: Fox/Photofest
76: © CORBIS SYGMA
78: Associated Press, AP/ KIM D. JOHNSON
80: Associated Press, AP/ CHRIS PIZZELLO
82: © Paramount Pictures/ ZUMA/CORBIS
85: Associated Press, AP/ NICK UT

COVER

AP Images

INDEX

ABOUT THE AUTHORS

RACHEL A. KOESTLER-GRACK has worked as an editor and writer since 1999. She has focused on historical topics, ranging from the Middle Ages to the Colonial era to the civil rights movement. In addition, she has written numerous biographies on a variety of historical and contemporary figures. Koestler-Grack lives with her husband and daughter on a hobby farm near Glencoe, Minnesota.

CHUCK D redefined rap music and hip-hop culture as leader and cofounder of legendary rap group Public Enemy. His messages addressed weighty issues about race, rage, and inequality with a jolting combination of intelligence and eloquence. A musician, writer, radio host, TV guest, college lecturer, and activist, he is the creator of Rapstation.com, a multiformat home on the Web for the vast global hip-hop community.